de

Vith

PER

Made

With PAPER

DRAGON'S WORLD

Florence Temko

Dragon's World Ltd
Limpsfield
Surrey RH8 0DY
Great Britain

First published by Dragon's World 1991

Art Editor Judith Robertson
Editor Angela Royston
Editorial Director Pippa Rubinstein

The catalogue record for this book is available from the British Library

ISBN 180528 152 1

Illustrator Susan Beresford
Photographer Ian Kalinowski

Printed in Singapore

Contents

Introduction

If you can cut with a pair of scissors and fold a crease, you are ready to make outstanding decorations, toys and gifts.

In *Made With Paper* I have assembled projects based on my experience in teaching many workshops and classes on paper arts and folk crafts. I find that most people like to make simple things that are useful and attractive, with reliable methods that produce good results, even the first time.

The book is divided into four sections: Mostly Cutting, Origami (Paperfolding), Pop-Ups and Constructions, and Papermaking. I decided to shape the book in this way, rather than by grouping according to specific purposes, such as greetings cards or table decorations, because I believe it offers you a greater variety.

For example, one day the cutting process for a star can give you a large, hanging ornament. The next time the same pattern can turn out several smaller stars which you can glue on a piece of stationery for a quick note to a sick friend. Another day you may be preparing for a party or a session of wrapping gifts.

You can skip through the pages and pick out as many ideas as may suit the occasion. On every page you will find suggestions for using your paper things as ornaments, gifts, bookmarks, home accessories and jewelry.

Mostly Cutting

For all the projects in this section you essentially need only one tool: a pair of scissors. Once you have cut out some paper gnomes or whatever else it may be, you can glue them to a greetings card, have them dance around a birthday cake or adapt them to your own needs.

Origami (Paperfolding)

For folding you do not even need scissors. The only required tools are your hands, yet you will be able to make many attractive decorations and toys. They are called 'models' in origami and appeal to children and adults alike. When paperfolders meet, everybody is in on the fun, ignoring age and language barriers.

Besides its practical aspects, many people find origami fascinating and pursue it as an all-consuming hobby for artistic, spiritual and aesthetic reasons.

Pop-Ups and Constructions

Add glue and a stapler and you are ready for this section which is full of surprises. Fastenings distinguish this section from Mostly Cutting.

Papermaking

Finally, in this section you can learn how to make your own sheets and decorate all kinds of papers. Some of the methods are hundreds of years old, but I have adapted them to the demands of today's lifestyle by simplifying them. You will be able to achieve quick results with the help of household materials which you may already own or can buy in local shops. Of the various methods shown for decorating paper you will probably enjoy dip-dyeing the most. When the paper is spread out to dry you will see the bold dramatic results of your own efforts.

In trying out these processes you will be working with beautiful papers, in what I hope is a pleasurable experience. A few among you may even become enthused about some aspect of papercrafting and explore further possibilities.

Interchanging Ideas

Paper is one of the most versatile materials. Do not be afraid to experiment by trying to apply a step used in one project to another project. You can only lose a piece of paper and perhaps you will come up with an idea that pleases you.

Paper as Art and Craft

Various papercrafting specialities and folkcrafts bloomed at different times and places. In Poland, when bright commercial papers became available, farm families began filling long winter hours by cutting layered papercuts into pictures of flowers, cockerels and other familiar subjects. In Scandinavia three-dimensional decorations were favoured, with a woven star being one of the most popular. In Mexico no fiesta would be complete without tissue papercuts strung across the street, and elaborate paper lanterns are featured at Filipino holidays.

Paperfolding (origami) and papercutting are the best-known oriental crafts which have now travelled to many other parts of the world. In accordance with Chinese funerary practices dating perhaps to 3500BC, household objects and other earthly goods were buried with deceased relatives to take care of their needs in the after-world as well as, or even better than, when they were alive. Paper replicas succeeded bronze and clay objects. They were also burned in temples for years after the death of an ancestor to ensure his or her goodwill.

The practice is frowned on in modern China, but is still practised in remote villages. I witnessed it in the Chinese community of Singapore several years ago. A large shop was stacked from floor to ceiling with the most amazing variety of paper goods available for this purpose: colourful furniture, carefully detailed automobiles, all kinds of farm animals, hand-painted robes and stacks of money. The handcrafting could only be envied and it seemed a pity that the objects were destined to be destroyed.

In the West, cutting paper with a penknife found royal favour beginning in the 16th century with Henri III (1551-89) of France. Of course, royal doings are always well documented and we know through researches at the Victoria and Albert Museum in London that English kings and queens collected papercuts and that Queen Anne (1665-1714) liked to cut paper herself.

In the 18th and 19th centuries silhouette cutting became very popular. Professional folk artists travelled in Europe and the United States, cutting portraits, birth and wedding certificates which were treasured in the family Bible. Amateur papercutting became a fashionable home entertainment.

Students at the German Bauhaus art and architecture school in the 1920s were asked to experiment with paper to bring out its innate qualities. This approach has had an enormous influence on paper designs.

The list could go on and on, because most countries have developed some sort of paper speciality besides those already mentioned.

History of Paper

The paper trail begins in China. Until recently its invention was attributed to an Imperial official, Tsai Lun, who combined bark, rags and hemp into paper. Reference to his achievement was recorded in official papers pinpointing the date to AD105. Unfortunately Tsai Lun's reputation as the first papermaker was undermined when paper scraps dating to 100 and even 200 years earlier were discovered by archeologists while excavating ancient tombs during the last two decades.

In the 7th century knowledge of papermaking began its migration from China, first to South-East Asia and later to Europe and America. Because of their country's climate and ample water resources, the Japanese developed highly sophisticated papermaking techniques. Paper touched many aspects of their lives, somewhat like plastics in our time. Paper was turned into window and door screens, clothing, lamps and other household needs. Some samurai armour was composed of layers of laminated papers formed over wooden forms. It was strong enough to deflect arrows.

Paper was highly regarded, even endowed with religious significance, to the extent that cutting paper was not permitted in ancient days. Folding did not violate its sacred spirit. In fact folding in prescribed ways became part of ritual ceremonies, which ultimately led to the development of elaborate gift wrapping and figurative origami.

Dard Hunter (1883-1966) was an American who devoted his life to the study of paper all over the world. He recorded his travels and research in several books. He made his own paper, cast the type and printed the books himself. They have since been republished commercially and are the most authoritative sources of information on papermaking techniques. Contemporary papermakers have contributed new scientific and technical information in more recent publications, as well as in art books which have been published illustrating their work.

The Institute of Paper Science and Technology in Atlanta, Georgia, is devoted entirely to the study of paper in all its aspects and includes the Dard Hunter Museum. Other museums which emphasize paper include the Paper Museum in Tokyo, the Cooper-Hewitt Museum in New York, the Mingei International Museum of World Folkcrafts in La Jolla, California, and, of course, the Victoria and Albert Museum in London.

Paper Manufacture

When paper was first invented, old rags, plant fibres and other materials formed the raw material. Now the main ingredient for commercial papers is wood pulp. High-grade papers still contain some rags because they provide desirable longer fibres. They are usually provided by fabric remnants collected at textile factories.

Until the 18th century all paper was made by hand. At that time machines began to facilitate the mass-production process. Enormous machines are now used in which the wood pulp is fed in at one end, floated over water, dried and rolled up into finished paper. Yet whether paper is made by hand or machine, the underlying principle of fibre formation has not changed since it was first established.

About Directions & Supplies

The instructions in this book are presented with text and illustrations. It is best to pay close attention to both, even to the extent of reading the words out loud. Yet some people respond better to words and others to visuals. For this reason I have tried to make the text complete in itself and the same with the illustrations, but let them help you in tandem to the clearest understanding.

Measurements

All dimensions are given in centimetres and inches. In order to avoid awkward fractions the sets of measurements may not always be exactly equal, but either set will work satisfactorily.

Key to Symbols

Cut

Crease paper up, called a valley fold

Crease paper to the back – away from you, called a mountain fold

Reverse fold

Thin line shows an existing crease made before

Arrow points the direction in which the paper is to be folded

Fold/unfold arrow: make a crease and unfold to the previous position

Turn the paper over from back to front

How to Cut a Square

1 Crease the corner of a sheet of paper in half, by bringing the short edge to the long edge.

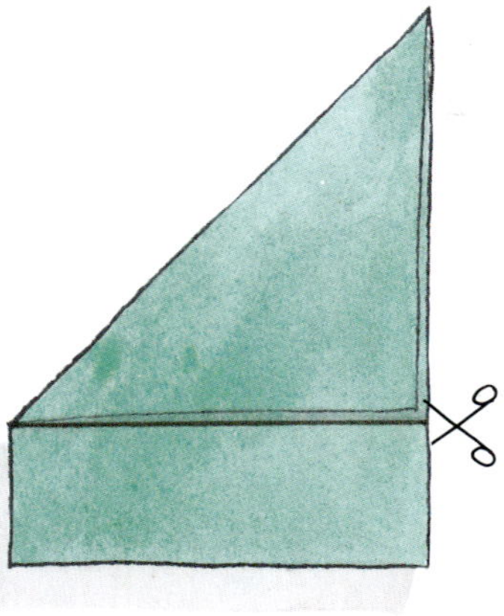

2 Cut off the single layer of paper.

3 Here is the square.

Papers

An infinite variety of papers exists which is wonderful but can be a little confusing. Suggestions for specific papers to use for each project are given throughout, but some general information may be helpful. Apart from colour, thickness of paper is probably of greatest importance and I will deal with both aspects in turn.

Coloured paper may be in solid colours or patterned, and can be divided into three kinds:

- Coloured on the front and white on the back, like giftwrap, some art papers and origami squares;
- Duo-coloured, with the same colour on the front and the back, like stationery;
- Duo-coloured, which is printed with different colours on the front and the back. You will find it in some art papers, a few giftwraps and some origami squares.

For some projects duo-colour is preferable because both sides of the paper appear in the final result.

In many projects I have suggested you use foil giftwrap. This is giftwrap which has a shiny coating of aluminium on one side only.

With regard to thickness, I should like to suggest three categories, without becoming too technical. Some projects may require thin paper because the final result might otherwise be too bulky. Other projects may require card to give them body.

- Thin papers: tissue paper, some giftwrap and origami squares, art papers, stationery, computer paper and foil giftwrap.
- Intermediate weight: Sugar (construction) paper, good quality writing paper, some handmade papers, art papers.

○ Card: Ingres (Strathmore), Canson Mi-teinte, thin cardboard, Bristol board, index cards, oaktag, posterboard, and some handmade papers.

Glues

Most glues you use generally can be used on paper. I am describing the ones I find most practical, but other kinds may serve you just as well. Because moisture buckles paper, it is most important to use only the smallest amount necessary for good adherence. Children particularly like to use glue liberally and it should be pointed out that they will achieve better results with very little. They usually understand perfectly, but have never been told before.

○ PVC and School Glue are referred to as white glue throughout and are most versatile. I usually spread a little on a piece of scrap paper and then apply it with the tip of my forefinger.

○ Rubber cement creates an easily removable bond when applied to one surface only and joined immediately to the other surface. It permits you to change your mind and rearrange designs. It can also be used for a permanent bond if you coat both surfaces and allow them to dry for a short time before pressing both surfaces together firmly. Any excess can be removed easily by rubbing it away with your fingers. Rubber cement is not recommended for work intended to last years and years, because it yellows and loses its adhesion after a time.

○ Spray glue is a form of rubber cement which is especially useful for bonding large pieces of paper together. Protect the working surface with newspaper and always work in a well-ventilated area. Children should be supervised.

○ Double-sided sticky tape and glue pens are other convenient means of gluing.

○ Duco-cement is useful for adhering paper to metal, such as earring fittings.

○ Wallpaper paste is a satisfactory and inexpensive adhesive especially suited for large projects.

Floral Wire

Floral wire is obviously useful with paper flowers but also for reinforcing standing forms. It comes in straight lengths and various thicknesses. It is more convenient than wire on rolls and comes in a few different varieties: plain, coated with green paint or plastic or with a fabric-like finish. It is available at florists and some craft shops and may be called stem or stub wire. You can cover plain wire with floral tape which stretches for good adherence. Attach wires to paper objects with sticky tape.

Where to Find Materials and Supplies

All projects can be made with materials from your nearest supermarket, stationers, art supply, museum store and other local shops. Larger cities offer a better selection of unusual papers and may even have a speciality paper store which will overwhelm you with choices. Giftwrap may turn up in the most unexpected places. Oriental outlets are often a good source for a large variety of origami squares and Japanese hand-made papers. For mail order contact:

In Great Britain:
Paperchase
213 Tottenham Court Road
London W1P 9AF
Phone: 071 580 8496
Contact for information and mail order for all kinds of paper and for glues.

Premier Book Marketing Ltd
1 Gower Street
London WC1E 6HA
Phone: 071 636 6005
Will supply by mail order origami squares and books on origami from their catalogue or give you details of your nearest retailer.

In the United States:
Dick Blick
P.O. Box 1267
Galesburg
Illinois 614-1267
Phone : 1-800-447-8192
Art materials suppliers offering a wide variety of papers by mail or through their stores. Ask for a catalogue.

Daniel Smith
Catalog of Artists' Material
4130 First Avenue South
Seattle WA 98134
Phone : 1-800-426-6940
Have a full selection of traditional and exotic papers from all over the world, but a minimum order of $25. Phone for a catalogue.

How to Contact Paperfolders

Origami is a popular hobby supported by groups in many different places. Paperfolders may meet on a regular or occasional basis, when beginners and experienced folders share information and designs about their hobby. The societies in Great Britain and the United States are very active and can put you in touch with other individual paperfolders and groups in many other countries. Ask about their supplies lists.

In Great Britain:
Dave Brill (Secretary)
British Origami Society
253 Park Lane
Poynton
Stockport
Cheshire SK12 1RH
Phone: 0625 872509

In the United States:
The Friends of the Origami Center of America
15 West 77th Street
New York NY 100244-5192
Phone: (212) 769-5635

Other Useful Information

Add-Ons
You can decorate the designs in *Made With Paper* with stickers, paper cutouts, left-over paper snips, glitter, confetti, feathers, ribbon, yarn and other odds and ends. Attach them with glue or double-sided sticky tape or a small closed loop made by winding ordinary sticky tape around two fingers.

Blank Cards
You can buy blank cards in stationery and art stores, or you can cut your own from card, or Ingres (Strathmore) or Canson Mi-teinte art paper. These usually not only offer a wider selection of colours, but work out to be cheaper. If you choose to make your own blank cards from fairly heavy card, it may be necessary to score the lines on which they are folded in half. Scoring is explained on page 13.

It is best to cut the card to fit the size of an available envelope rather than try to find an envelope to fit the card. If you like you can make an envelope as shown on page 21. In either case the finished, folded card should be about ½cm (¼in) narrower and shorter than the envelope so it slides in easily.

Children's Papercrafting
Children can really enjoy most of the projects, but at all times adults should first familiarize themselves with the directions to ensure that they are within the capabilities of the children involved. Papercrafts are fun as a family activity for parents and children to explore together. Older children will be able to proceed on their own, subject to adult guidance. With larger youth groups and in schools it is best to prepare yourself by trying out the activity before presenting it. (See also Parties and Teaching.)

Cutting
When cutting curves always hold the hand with the scissors still and move the paper into the scissors. This assures smooth lines. It may seem awkward at first, but will become a habit in a short time.

Collecting
Like other hobbyists, papercrafters enjoy collecting samples and books on their favourite subject. They house designs in cardboard boxes and plastic containers. It is a good idea to store similar items under group headings such as Greetings cards, Holidays, Folkcraft, Animals, and so on.

In a more ambitious scheme you can store individual designs alphabetically by placing each item in a transparent envelope together with a card detailing the name and other comments. In this way you form a ready reference library in case you want to repeat or display items at a later date.

Folding
Although a whole section of the book is devoted to origami, here are some suggestions about folding which apply throughout.

Always make sharp creases by folding on a hard surface. It helps to confirm the crease with your fingernail or a folding 'bone', which can be a ruler, an icecream stick or similar tool. The more accurate your creases, the better the final result.

When working on complex designs a slight inaccuracy in the shape of the beginning square of paper can cause problems later on.

Young children should fold only very simple things which do not require extreme accuracy. For example when asking them to make a diagonal fold on a square say: 'Let one corner kiss the other corner. Pat the long crease.' They will recognize the shape as a triangle or boat.

Gift Wrapping
With all the ideas you find in *Made With Paper* imaginative gift wrapping becomes easy. Attach almost any of the designs to the top of a package and you will be known for your flair.

Jewelry
Many of the paper things can be made in a small size and used as jewelry. Craft stores carry brooch and pin backs, and fittings for pierced and non-pierced ears, some of which are shown in the illustration. Earrings may also be hung with loops of thread. If gluing is indicated, use Duco-cement or other strong glue. (See also Laminating.)

Laminating
You can laminate two pieces of paper together to create duo-coloured paper with extra stability. Spray-glue is easiest to handle, but other glues will do. Foil giftwrap bonded to regular paper becomes stronger and more workable. Because it is difficult to laminate the edges of two pieces exactly evenly, follow these steps.

1 Cut two pieces of paper in the desired colours at least 1cm (½in) larger all round than the final piece you need.
2 Place one piece white side up. Spray or spread glue lightly all over.
3 Place the other piece on top, white side down. Press evenly all over.

4 Let the paper dry for a few minutes. Cut it into the desired size.

Some photocopy shops offer a laminating service in which the paper is covered with a clear varnish-like cover. You may want to consider this service for covering paper for boxes, wallets and jewelry. (See also Protective Coatings.)

Layering

Interesting effects are possible by using two or three layers of paper instead of one. Use different colours and make one layer extend outside the other. For example, you could cut stars (see pages 50 to 56) in this way. Cut two stars the same size in two different colours. Cut off ½cm (¼in) all around one of them.

Mobiles

Because of its light weight, paper is a perfect material for decorations which can be suspended from the ceiling, as Christmas tree ornaments or over a baby's crib. Any air current in the room, whether from a window or radiator, will move them gently. I like to use fishing line, which blends in with any colour, to hang the pieces. Knot a loop of fishing line to the mobile in two places. Attach another length to this loop for hanging. This can be shifted on the loop to balance the ornament evenly.

Mobiles with multiple figures are very attractive but I find their construction quite time-consuming and prefer to hang single pieces. The peace crane (see page 82), made from a 40cm (15in) square, is one of my favourite gifts for a new baby.

Paper Engineering

Pop-up books were invented in Victorian times, but disappeared after a period of popularity. Lately they have been revived and with them the new craft of paper engineering. The pop-up greetings card (see page 95) is a very simple example, but designers invent quite ingenious three-dimensional scenes that pop forward, peepholes, mouths that open and close and pull-tabs that make animals appear and disappear.

Paper Sizes

Standard A4 letter paper measures 10mm by 297mm. US letter paper measures 8½in by 11in.

Parties

Whether for adults or children you will find plenty of ideas for making party favours and toys throughout the book. They can be made ahead of time or at the party. The fancy hat, the woven basket and the magic wand are obvious choices. On the other hand, the children can make their own favours at the party, in this way providing their own entertainment.

For a successful party, provide colourful papers, felt-tip pens and add-ons, like stickers and metallic confetti. Arrange them in boxes on a table and let guests make their own selections.

In addition to providing these supplies, you must prepare yourself by learning how to make two or three things until you can do them automatically. Teach the children one of them step-by-step. Then let them experiment. You will be able to judge when they are ready for the next idea. Once they get into the spirit they will come up with their own ideas. (See also Add-Ons and Teaching.)

Pleating

Pleating is one of the easiest ways to add interesting surface treatment to a piece of paper, whether it is called 'fan' or 'accordion' pleating. The paper should be at least two and a half times as long as it is wide. Even pleats may be achieved with three different methods. The first one is my favourite.

Method 1 Establish preliminary creases for eight pleats by folding the paper into 16 equal parts like this: fold the paper in half, in half again and again a third and fourth time. After the first or second time it may become difficult to fold all the layers together. Use the existing creases to guide you in folding only half the layers. When all these creases are established, some will be up and others down in random fashion. Unfold the paper to its full length. Crease the paper alternately up and down on the lines.

For longer strips which need more than eight pleats, you can still use this method. Use the guidelines and follow the suggestion for folding as many layers as make a convenient bundle. You will end up with 16 or 24 pleats.

Method 2 You need a ruler and pencil. Mark the paper lightly where creases are to be made. In this case decide on the width of the pleats, which usually varies between 1cm and 3cm (½in and 1in), depending on the size of the fan. Rather than draw a complete line for each crease, make light pencil marks near both long edges of the paper which will be less visible in the end. If the paper does not end with an even pleat, cut off the left-over piece.

Method 3 Again you need a ruler and pencil. Calculate the width of the pleats first by dividing the length of the paper into an even number. For example, if the paper is 50cm (20in) long you could decide on ten 2½cm (1in) pleats. Then mark the paper lightly near the top and bottom of the long edges.

Protective Coatings

Paper objects can be coated for longer life. Acrylic sprays offer the lightest protection and barely change the appearance. White glue (PVC) spread on in one or more coats dries clear. Other synthetic finishes and varnishes are sold in do-it-yourself, paint, art supply and hardware shops. They can be brushed on or small objects can be dipped into the container while being suspended on a piece of wire or a paperclip bent open.

It is best to enquire at the shops which products are available, because new ones appear all the time and old ones disappear. Look for quick-drying liquid plastic finishes which dry clear and are non-yellowing. Some of them give a hard glass-like finish, which is especially appropriate for jewelry and decoupage. Always test a product on a spare piece of paper before applying it to a finished piece of work.

You can also protect paper with sticky-back plastic (clear self-adhesive plastic sheeting). Buy it in rolls or find a photocopy shop which offers laminating services. Sticky-back plastic is most suitable for covering paper boxes, wallets and jewelry. (See also Laminating.)

Recycling

Paper is an environmentally sound material. Wood fibre, the main ingredient of paper, is a renewable resource, because lumber companies are learning to manage the growth and harvesting of trees. To complete the cycle, old newspaper, magazines and outdated letters are collected and turned into fresh paper supplies or building materials. Some materials carry a circular symbol, indicating that they are recycled.

The paper recycling business is attracting some innovative technologies, and, if you make paper as shown in this book, you are part of this process in its simplest form.

Scoring

Paper and lightweight card can be folded neatly, but with heavier card a crease may crack unevenly. This can be avoided by scoring, which means cutting halfway through the thickness of the paper with a craft knife. In company with many others, I do not like scoring and try to avoid it, but this is how it is done.

Protect the working surface against cuts and scratches by covering it with a thick layer of newspaper or a magazine. Mark the line to be scored lightly in pencil. Place a metal ruler on the line and guide a craft knife along its edge. The pressure should be such that the paper is not cut all the way through. You will soon discover the right amount of pressure needed and that you have to press a little harder at the beginning and end of the cut.

Fold away from the score, leaving the cut on the outside of the card.

Squares

Many projects, including most of the origami models, specify the use of paper squares. You can measure the sides, using a ruler and a drafting square, but an easier way is shown under Directions and Supplies on page 8.

Teaching

Papercraft is a wonderful educational tool which is becoming more and more recognized by teachers. It is fun yet satisfies educational objectives in mathematics, art, language and social studies. It aids co-ordination between hands and eyes and crosses interdisciplinary and multi-cultural boundaries.

Whenever you are teaching, whether it is an individual, a class or any other group, familiarize yourself thoroughly with every aspect of a project before presenting it. You may wish to utilize some of the wording used in my instructions which I have tried to make as clear as possible. Encourage students to craft with paper in their own time and to innovate variations in designs.

Washi Paper

This is a soft Japanese handmade paper in solid colours, or stencilled and decorated, sometimes with breathtaking designs. It may be found in some art supply, speciality and oriental stores. Choose it for really exquisite results, because it will always enhance your work. Some traditional washi designs are copied on machine-made paper with a harder surface and at a lower cost.

Mostly Cutting

Cutting paper seems to be an instinctive pleasure. At an early age most children like to snip paper into small pieces. Before long they design pictures by pasting the shapes on to a background. This can keep them occupied for a very long time, far beyond their usual concentration span.

In this section I am trying to extend the same kind of enjoyment in papercutting to older children and to adults. Most designs are pure cutting, but they may be glued or combined in other ways for decorations and other practical purposes.

Always use sharp scissors. Safety scissors designed for children are available, but most young children can handle scissors competently when they are supervised and taught to use them properly. Always hand scissors to another person by holding the closed blades and extending the handles.

Cutting straight lines requires no special advice, but train yourself to cut curves by holding the scissors stationary and feeding the paper into the scissors with the other hand. After a little practice this movement becomes automatic and produces smooth curves.

Hearts Wall Frieze

A wall frieze can be made from computer paper, shelf paper or left-over wallpaper and decorated with simple cutouts. It may be used as a semi-permanent fixture or as a temporary decoration for birthday parties or in meeting rooms for special events.

You will need:

Origami paper, 15cm (6in) square
Tracing paper or photocopy (see below)
Pencil, scissors, ruler, glue
Continuous computer paper, or shelf paper
Masking tape or magic tape

1 Fold the square into quarters by folding it in half one way then in half the other way.

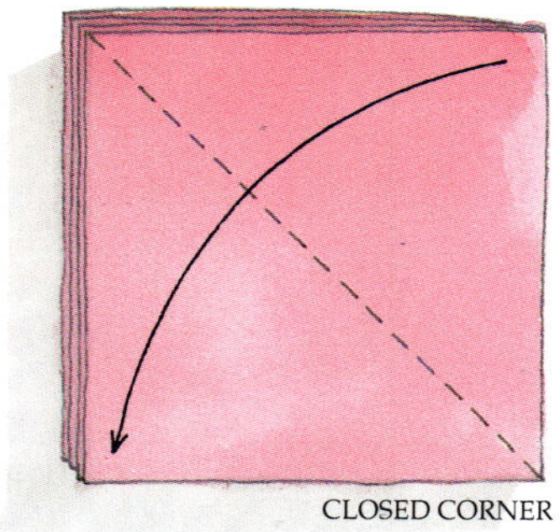

2 You now have a smaller square. One corner is 'closed'. This is the centre of the paper. Fold from this corner along the diagonal. Now you have a triangle.

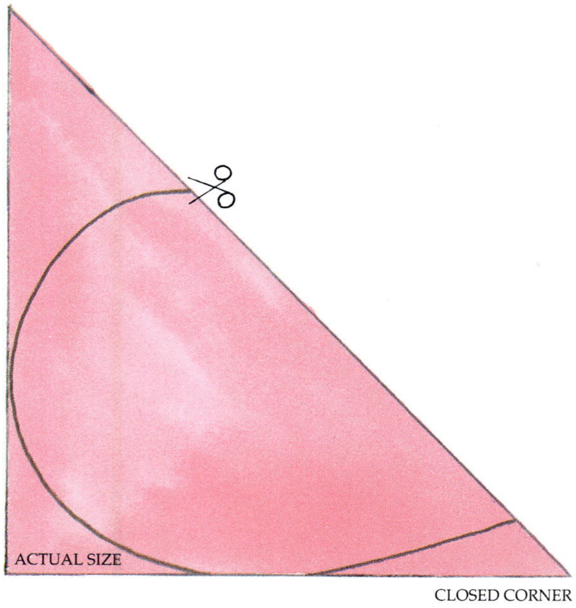

3 Trace or photocopy the curved lines for the heart shape.

4 Cut it out and place it over the folded triangle. Make sure the closed corner is exactly where shown. Cut on the lines.

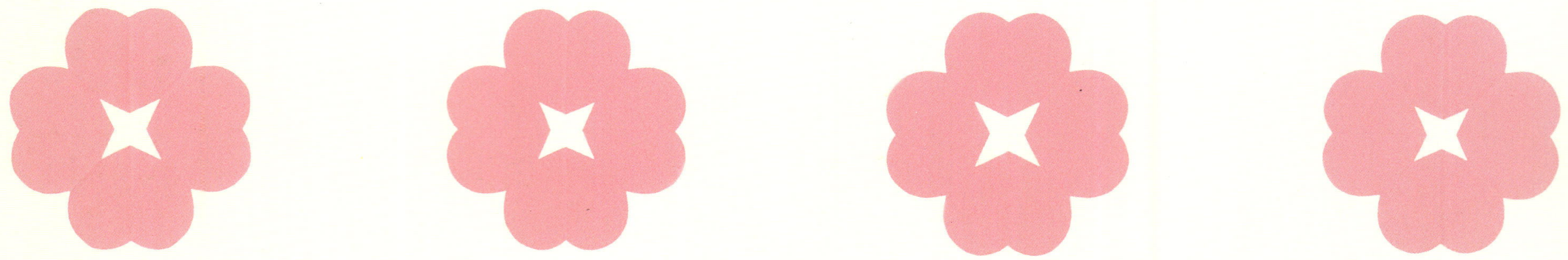

5 Open the paper flat.

6 To make the wall frieze, lay out as many continuous sheets of computer paper as you need for the length. Count the number of pages and cut one four-heart design for each page. Use a ruler to find the centre of each page and glue one design at the centre of each. (If you are using shelf paper, glue one design every 28cm (11in).) Attach the frieze in place with masking tape or with magic tape which is transparent and does not take the paint off when you remove it.

Other Sizes

Glue smaller heart designs onto narrower strips of paper.

Star Cutting Frieze

Did you notice that the fall-off from the centre formed a star and the surround a flower-shaped frame? You can use them to make another frieze or for decorating stationery and greetings cards.

Multi-Coloured Hearts

Decorate the four hearts with smaller hearts or other cutouts.

Patchwork Star Card

Paper can be patchworked together to make greetings cards which simulate quilting. This Christmas star card is made only with a square and triangles.

You will need:

A blank card 18cm by 12½cm (7in by 5in)
– see page 11
Gold paper or other shiny paper
Scissors, glue

1 Cut a 5cm (2in) square from the gold paper.

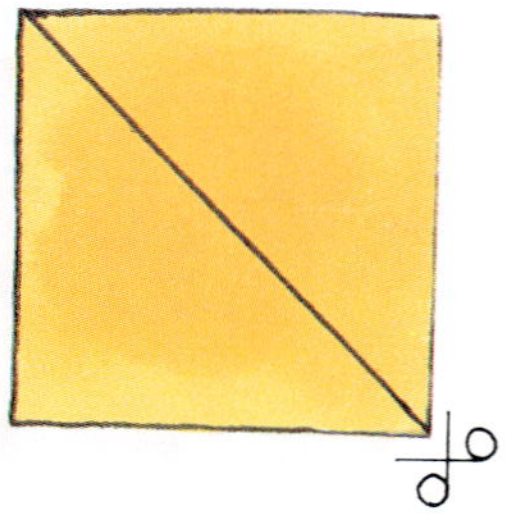

2 Cut four 2½cm (1in) squares from the gold paper. Then cut them along the diagonal into eight triangles.

3 Glue the large square in the middle of the card. Glue the eight triangles around it as shown.

Basket Card

This card is made from patchwork like the star card. It uses triangles cut from two different colours or patterns of paper.

You will need:

A blank card 18cm by 12½cm (7in by 5in)
– see page 11
Paper in two different colours or patterns
Tracing paper
Pencil, scissors, glue

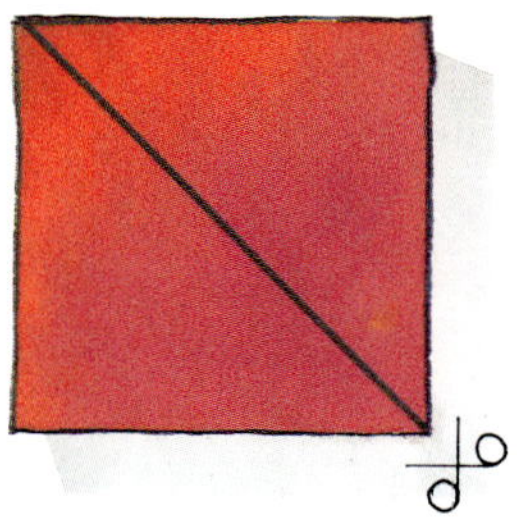

1 Cut three 2½cm (1in) squares from each colour. Cut them into triangles along the diagonal.

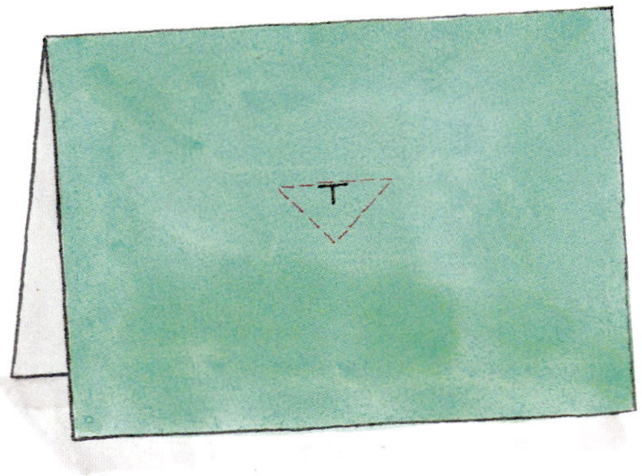

2 Find the middle of the top edge by lightly marking in pencil 9cm (3½in) from one side. Measure down 5cm (2in) from this point and make a short pencil line. Glue on a triangle as shown by the dotted lines.

3 This is the middle triangle in the top row. Paste the other triangles as.shown.

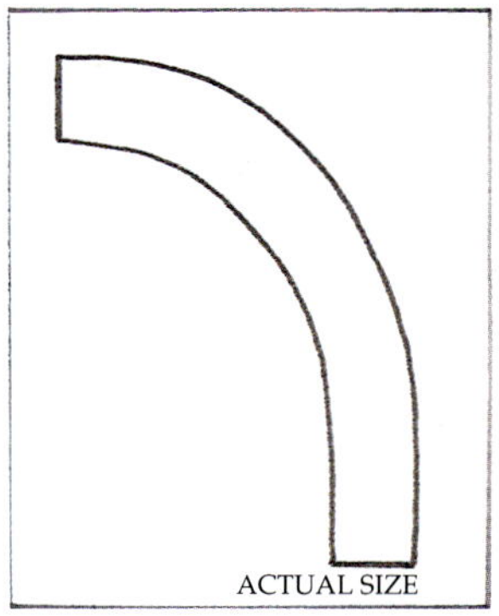

4 Trace the half-pattern for the handle.

5 Fold a piece of coloured paper in half. Place the handle pattern against the folded edge. Cut out the handle through the tracing paper and double layer of coloured paper.

6 Glue it on the card. You can cut flowers from giftwrap and glue them on too.

More Patchwork Patterns

Now you can experiment with your own patchwork designs. Stick left-over scraps of coloured paper and giftwrap on to blank cards to make your own supply of unique cards.

You will need:

Blank cards (see page 11)
Several scraps of coloured paper and giftwrap with small patterns
Pencil, scissors, ruler, glue

1 Cut several squares and triangles from different scraps of paper. Also cut several strips ½cm (¼in) wide but to different lengths.

2 Lay the pieces of paper onto the card, starting at the centre and working outwards. When you are happy with your pattern, glue the pieces down.

3 Experiment by adding rectangles made from squares cut in half. Leave spaces between the pieces. Mix larger and smaller squares and triangles.

Posters

Make posters and pictures in the same way as greetings cards, using larger squares, triangles and other geometric shapes.

Quicky Envelope

When you would like to match an envelope to the paper used in a greetings card, you can make this simple one from a paper square. In order for the written address to show up clearly, it is best to use light-coloured paper. Nevertheless on darker paper you can paste on a label or use a pen with white or silver ink.

You will need:

A piece of paper 26cm (11in) square makes an envelope about 18½cm by 15cm (7¼in by 6in)
Ruler, pencil, sticky tape

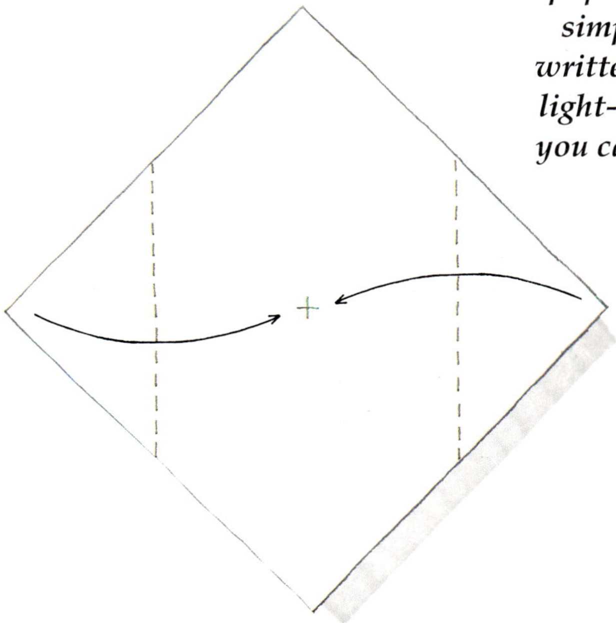

1 Measure and mark the centre of the paper lightly with a pencil. Fold two opposite corners to the mark.

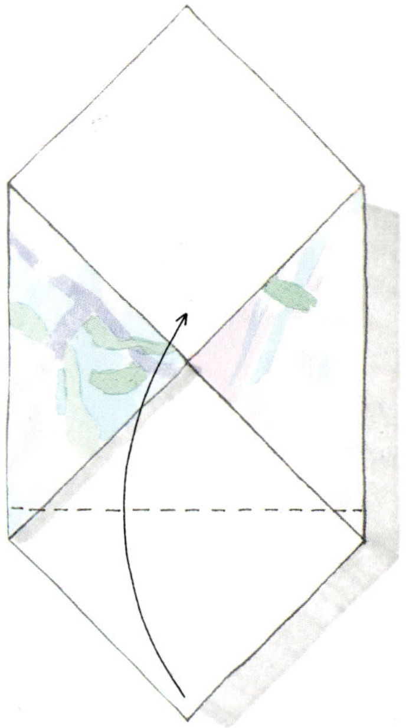

2 Fold the bottom corner up taking in about 1½cm (¾in) of the folded edges.

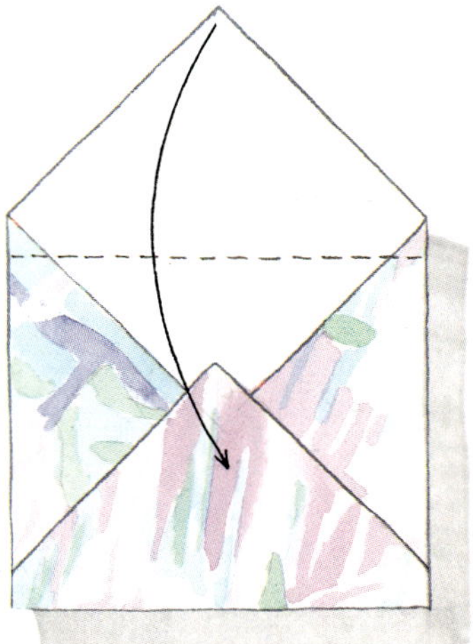

3 Fold the top down taking in about 1½cm (¾in) of the folded edges.

4 Seal the corner of the envelope with sticky tape. For posting, it is best to seal all the edges with sticky tape, so that they do not get caught in Post Office machinery.

Dancing Teddy Bear

For centuries the Dancing Teddy has delighted us. Hang him on the wall where anyone can make him perform at the pull of the string.

You will need:

Coloured card
Tracing paper or photocopy (see below)
Four double-pronged paper fasteners
Strong thread and needle
Coloured paper or thin card for clothes and accessories
Pencil, scissors, felt-tip pen, glue

1 Trace the five pattern pieces (or photocopy them). Place the tracing, or photocopy, on top of the card. Cut out the five pieces through the paper and card. Copy all the features, X's and O's with a felt-tip pen.

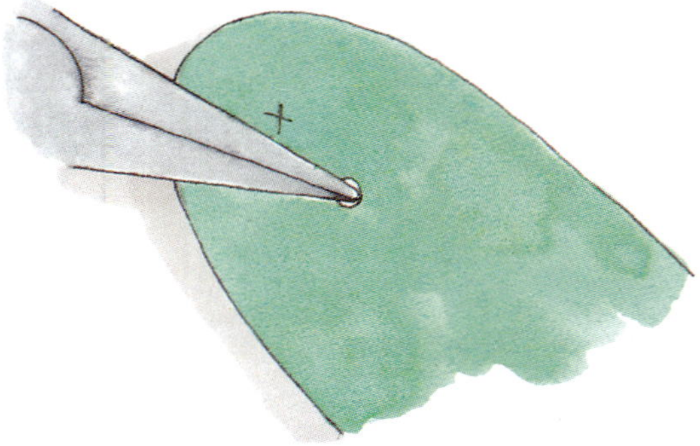

2 Pierce holes at the O's with the points of the scissors. Attach the arms and legs behind the body with paper fasteners through the O holes. The heads of the fasteners will be in front. Make sure the limbs move easily; if not, then loosen the fasteners.

Other Toys

You can easily make other toys. Draw your own simple outline of a clown, monkey or other favourite animal or person. Decorate it and assemble it as for the Dancing Teddy Bear.

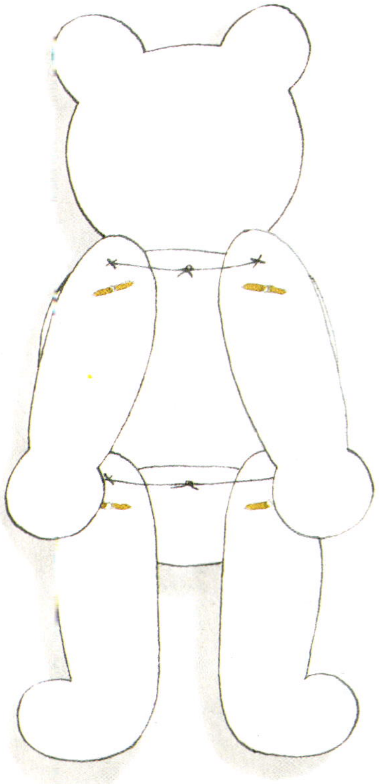

3 Attach the string mechanism to the back. Let the limbs hang straight down. Push the thread through the X on one arm and across to the X on the other arm. Tie into a loop with a knot.

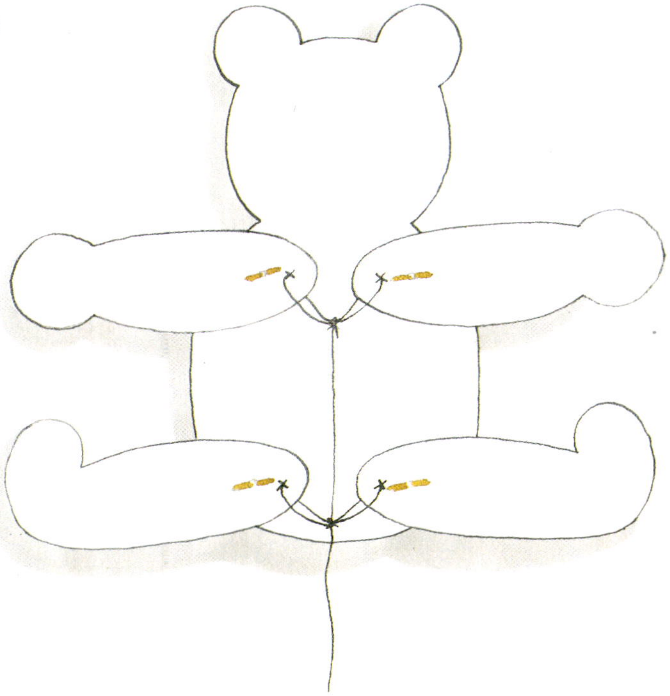

4 Thread the legs together in the same way.

5 Cut a 60cm (25in) length of thread. Knot the long string round the middle of the arm and leg loops.

6 You can clothe Teddy in the waistcoat or dress and basket. Trace or photocopy them, or design your own hats and clothes. Cut them from stiff coloured paper or thin card and stick them on Teddy.

7 Glue a loop of thread to the top of the head. Hold Teddy at the top or hang him on the wall. Pull down the string at the bottom to make him dance.

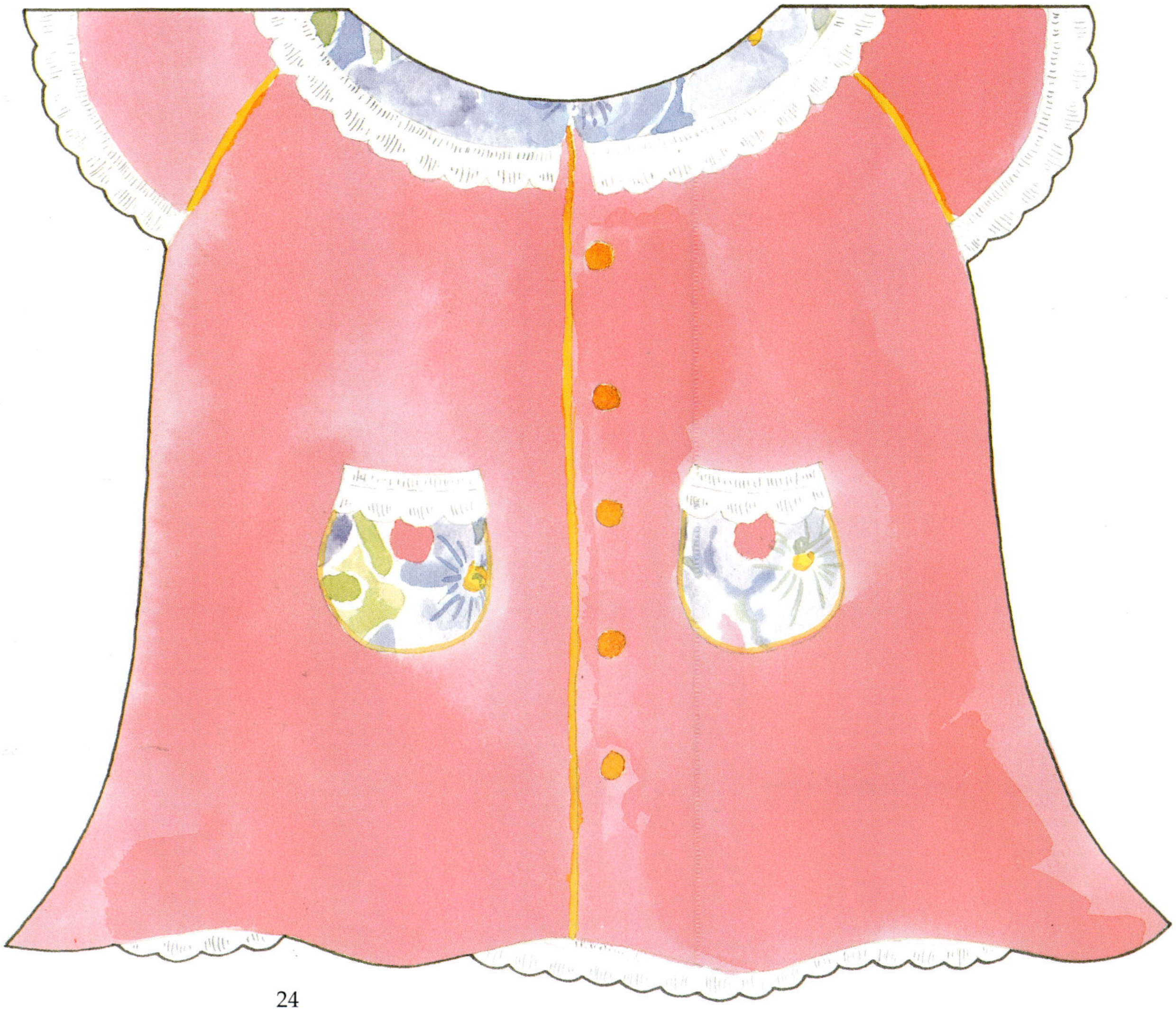

Shadow Portraits

Shadow portraits, or silhouettes, were a way of providing a personal likeness before photography was invented. Today you can make them for special family occasions, at local fairs and as a fun activity.

You will need:

Paper that is black on one side and white on the other (see note on paper on right)
Pencil, scissors, masking tape, glue
Lamp or slide projector
White card

1 Choose a wall, window, board or other vertical flat surface that cannot be damaged by masking tape. Tape on the paper with the white side facing out.

2 Seat the person whose portrait is to be cut close to the paper with his or her head turned sideways. Place the light source so that a shadow of the head appears. Move the light until the shadow is sharp.

3 Draw a pencil line round the edge of the shadow. Remove the paper from the background.

4 Cut along the pencil line. To get a good result, cut all curves by moving the hand that is holding the paper, and keep the hand with the scissors still.

5 Lightly glue the black silhouette onto a white background. Silhouettes look very effective on a window pane, or framed.

Paper

Shadow portraits are best cut from paper that is black on one side and white on the other. Special silhouette paper is sold in art supply shops. Black giftwrap and other kinds of paper can also be used. If these are not available, then cut the silhouette from white paper and glue it onto a black background.

Tissue-Paper Garlands

You can add instant festive atmosphere to adult and children's parties with tissue-paper garlands. Cut them quickly from pleated paper. Then attach them with masking tape, high up along a wall, over a doorway or across a corner of the room.

You will need:

A sheet of tissue paper
75cm by 52cm (30in by 20in)
Pencil, scissors, sticky tape

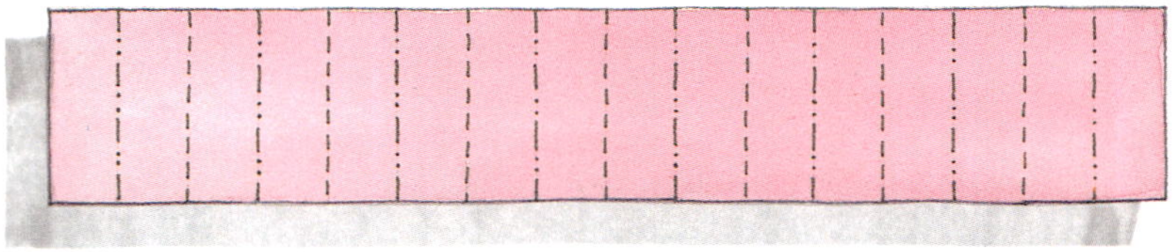

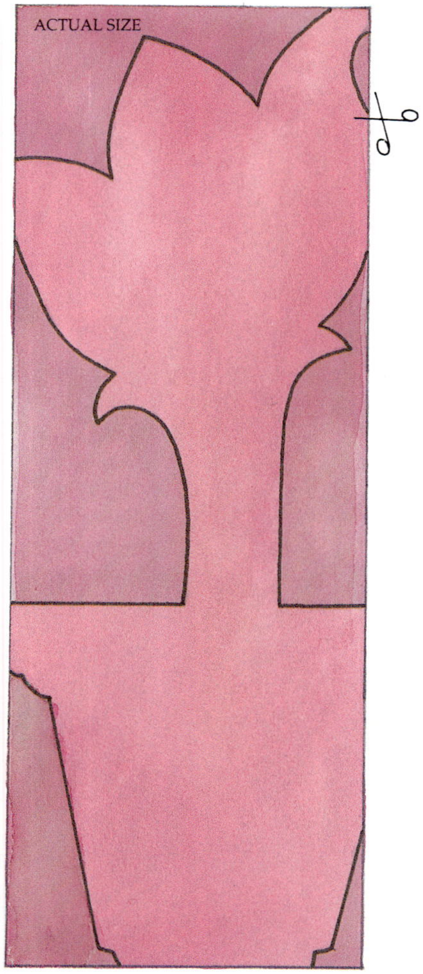

1 Fold a sheet of tissue paper into quarters lengthwise and cut into four long strips.

2 Fold one strip into 16 parts by folding it in half four times.

3 Choose one of the designs shown and draw it onto the folded strip. Cut along the lines. Note that the design leaves parts of the side edges. If all of one side is cut away the garland falls apart.

4 Open up the strip. You now have a completed section of garland. Do the same with the other three strips and tape them together to form one long garland.

Two-Colour Garland

Cut strips of tissue paper in a contrasting colour, but do not cut out the pattern. Glue the patterned strip onto the contrasting strip.

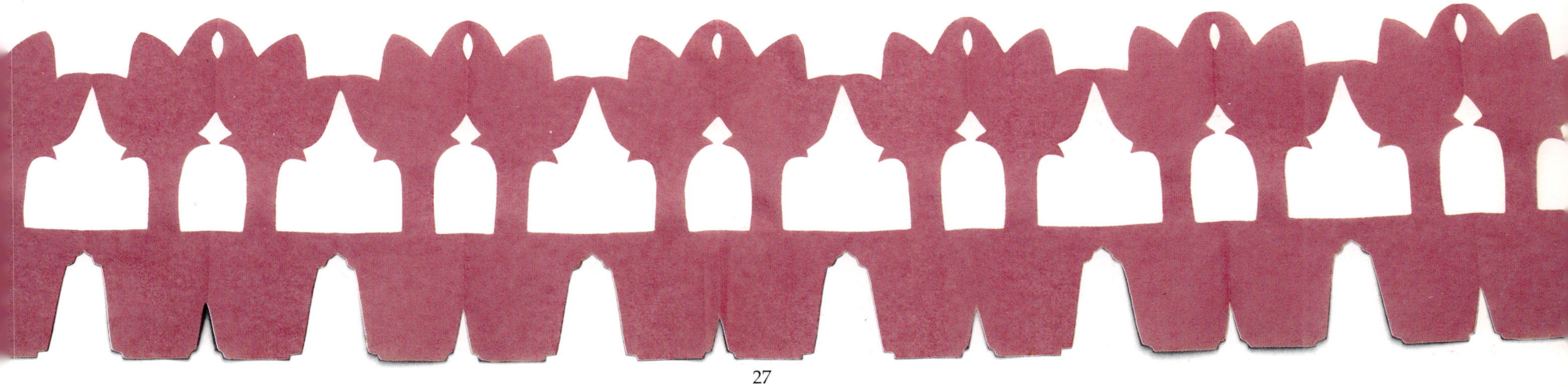

Gnomes Christmas Decoration

In a traditional Danish Christmas decoration a paper tree is surrounded by red dancing gnomes, called nissors. This decoration can grace the dinner table or the gnomes may be spread in a row on the mantelpiece in front of the paper tree. Coloured papers available from photocopy shops are a good weight to use.

You will need:

Four A4 sheets of green paper
Red paper
Tracing paper
or photocopy (see below)
Pencil, scissors,
glue, ruler

Christmas Tree

1 Fold the four sheets of green paper in half lengthwise. Unfold and lay them one on top of the other. Glue the sheets together in the middle, by spreading narrow lines of glue on the creases between the sheets. Let them dry.

2 Fold all four sheets together in half. Trace or photocopy the tree. Place the tracing paper on top of the glued papers with the straight edge to the fold. Cut the sides of the tree through all the layers of paper. (If the paper is too thick, leave the sheets unfolded and copy the tree outline onto the right and left sides of the top sheet. Then cut each side separately.)

3 Separate the layers of paper and crease close to the middle, forming a three-dimensional tree.

Gnomes

1 Cut a strip of red paper 50cm by 10cm (20in by 4in). (Tape two shorter pieces together, if necessary.) Fold into eight sections by folding the strip in half three times.

2 Trace or photocopy the gnome. Staple the tracing paper or photocopy on top of the folded paper outside the design. Cut out the gnome through all the layers. Note the side edges are left uncut at the hands and the feet – otherwise the gnomes separate. Unfold the paper.

3 Tape the ends together and arrange the gnomes in a circle so that they dance around the tree.

Christmas Tree

You can use the tree by itself, topping it with a little gold star or adding other decorations. You can also use it with one or two of the reindeer shown on page 106 to make a decorative Christmas scene.

Gnome Stationery

Glue one or more gnomes on to your letters to give them a more festive air.

Cake Garland

The fold-and-cut method used for the gnomes on page 28 can be adapted to all kinds of other figures. Here are two examples. One makes into a row of kittens to go around a birthday cake for a cat-lover. The other makes a garland of gorillas for a zoo theme.

1 Pleat the paper as you did in step 1 of the gnomes on page 28.

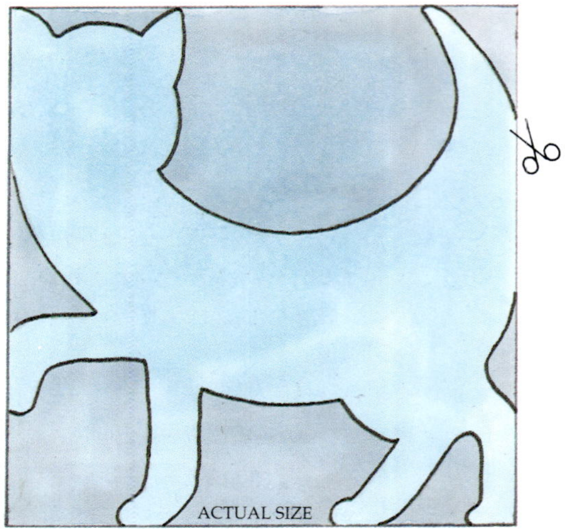

You will need:

Coloured A4 sheets or giftwrap with a small pattern
Pencil, scissors, sticky tape

2 Trace or photocopy the outline of the kitten or gorilla. Staple the photocopy to the paper and cut through all the layers, as in step 2 of the gnomes. Note that the kittens are connected at the head, feet and tail, and so these parts must remain uncut. The gorillas are joined at the arms.

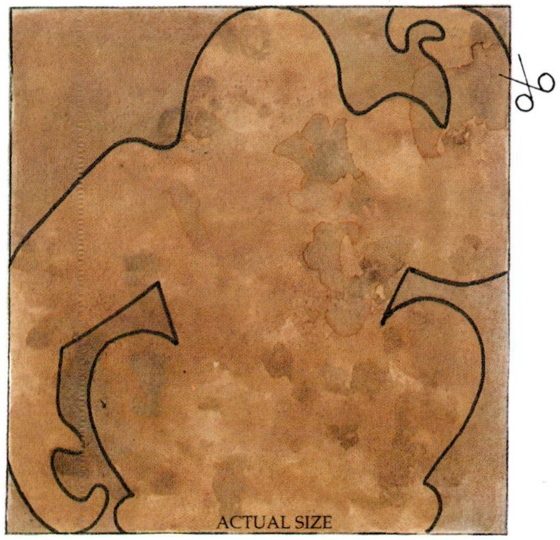

3 Place the garland round the cake and tape the ends together.

Giftwraps & Other Fan Pleatings

With the simplest kind of pleating you can create unique gift packages and many other decorations.

You will need:

Giftwrap or other coloured paper
Scissors, ruler, pencil
Stapler or sticky tape
Double-sided sticky tape

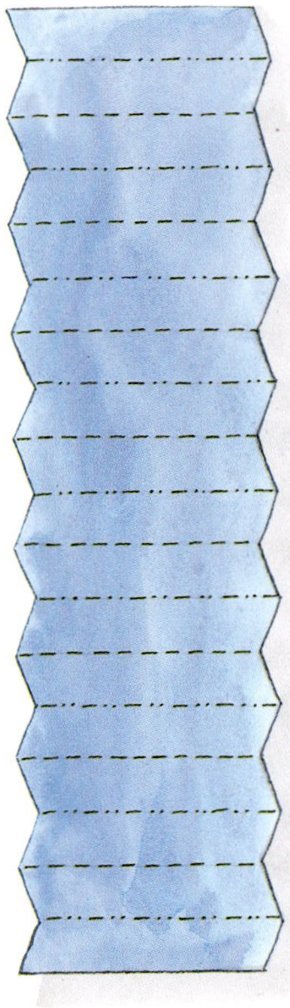

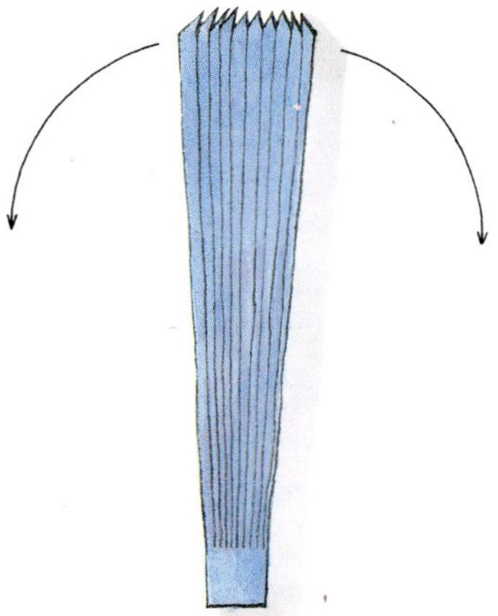

1 Cut a piece of paper about four times as long as it is wide – for example, 6cm by 25cm (2½in by 10in). Make light pencil marks at 1cm (½in) intervals along the paper and pleat it into a fan.

2 Staple or wind a piece of narrow sticky tape tightly round one end of the fan. Spread out the other end.

3 Tape the fan to a package with double-sided sticky tape.

Circle Fan

For a complete circle, pleat a fan from a strip of paper that is seven times as long as it is wide. Tape the end pleats together.

Striped Paper

The illustration shows the surprising result you get when you make a circle fan from striped paper.

Oversize

It is sometimes difficult to find decorations which are big enough to make an impression in a big hall or auditorium. Oversize circle fans can be made from very large pieces of giftwrap or other paper. They can be folded up for transporting and opened up quickly on location.

Valentine Gift

A Valentine's Day giftwrap can be made with a very ordinary kind of paper. When you fold a circle fan with computer paper, the holes on the edges provide the customary lacy look.

You will need:

3 sheets of continuous computer paper
Red or pink giftwrap
Scissors, double-sided sticky tape

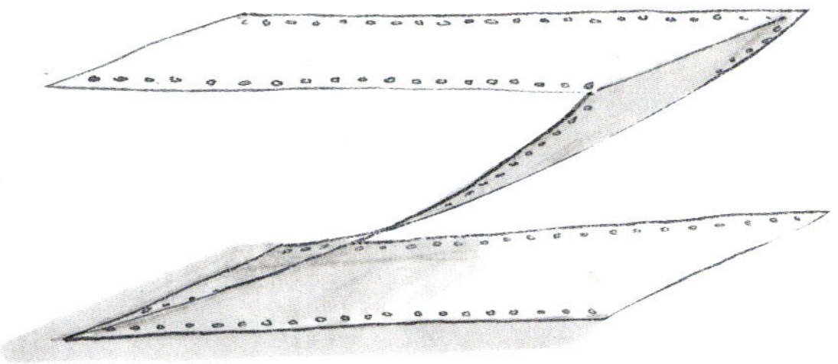

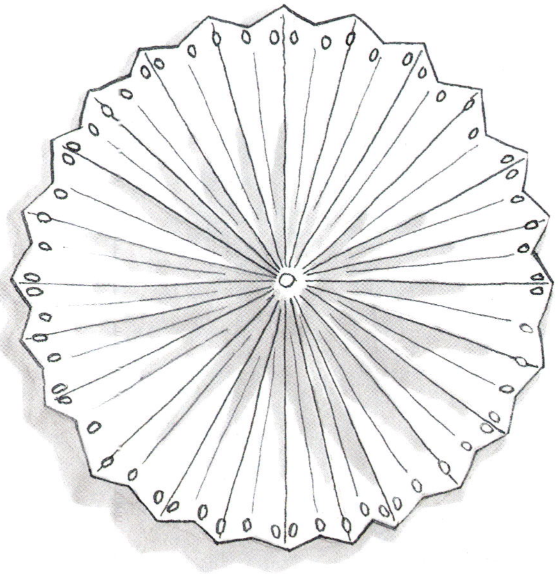

1 Lay three sheets of connected computer paper one on top of the other. Cut of a strip lengthwise which is 8cm (3in) wide.

2 Fold one of the strips into a circle fan (see page 31). Be careful the perforated edge does not tear off.

3 Wrap the gift in red or pink paper. Detach the edge from the other strip of computer paper and wind it around the package near the top and the bottom. Tape at the back with double-sided sticky tape.

4 Attach the fan to the package with double-sided sticky tape.

5 Cut out a red or pink heart and glue it to the centre of the fan.

Fancy Fan

This fancy fan is another variation on the circle fan shown on page 31. Make it in contrasting paper to make an unusual decoration for a giftwrapped box.

You will need:

A piece of giftwrap 6cm by 42cm
(2½in by 17½in)
Scissors, sticky tape, stapler

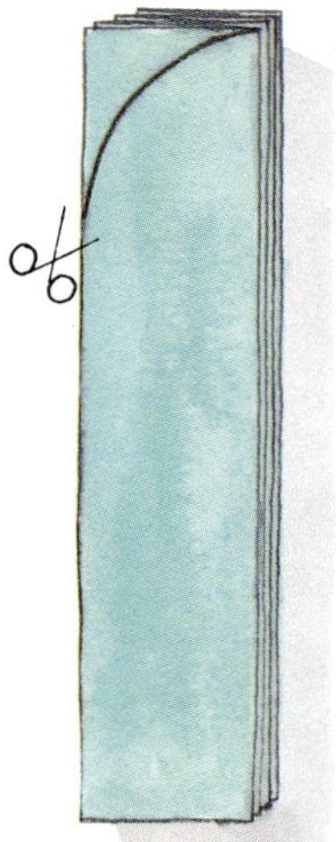

1 Fold a circle fan with the giftwrap. Tape the bottom of the fan as instructed in step 2 of the basic fan on page 31. Cut a curve at the top of each pleat to give a scalloped edge.

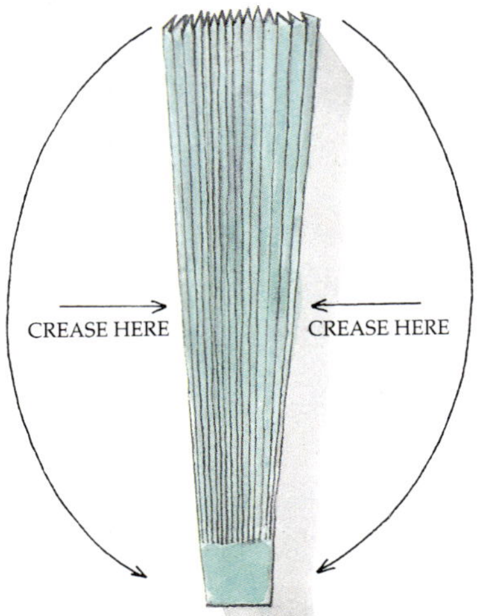

2 On both sides of the fan, grasp the top of the end pleat and tape or staple it to the bottom of the fan. The fan spreads out as you do this.

3 Before taping the fancy fan to the wrapped box, cut several strips of giftwrap. Tape them to the middle of the package.

Party Rosette

Attach circle fans to straws and you have instant party toys. Children will love to open and close them or carry them in a parade. Use brightly coloured paper, or black and white paper for a note of elegant fun at an adult party. Because rosettes collapse securely, they can be taken to a picnic and stuck to the sides of a picnic basket.

You will need:

Tissue paper or cellophane
Cardboard
A wide drinking straw
Scissors, stapler, sticky tape

1 Cut a piece of tissue paper 8cm by 56cm (3in by 22in). Fold it into a fan (see page 31).

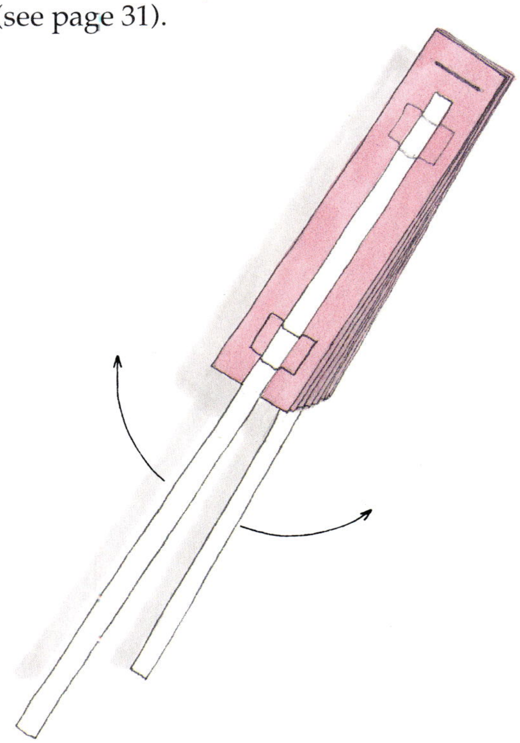

2 Cut two narrow strips of cardboard about 20cm (8in) long and slightly narrower than the straw. Tape them to the outsides of the fan. Note the ends are placed about 1cm (½in) away from the stapled end of the fan.

3 Open the fan and insert the cardboard in the straw.

4 To make a more decorative rosette, cut the edge of the fan with pinking shears while it is still folded.

Magic Wand

When you attach a rosette to a dowel stick, it becomes a magic wand. You can give it as a present as an unusual alternative to flowers, chocolates or a birthday card. At Christmas you can arrange several magic wands made from foil giftwrap on a mantlepiece.

You will need:

Tissue paper
Cardboard
A dowel stick
Paper streamers
Scissors, stapler, sticky tape

1 Make a circle fan and glue the outsides to cardboard strips as described in steps 1 and 2 of the party rosette.

2 Open the fan and tape the cardboard strips to a dowel stick.

3 Knot some ribbon streamers just below the rosette. You can add a card with an appropriate message, for example: 'Happy Birthday! May this magic wand make all your wishes come true'.

Parallel-Cut Napkin Ring

Making parallel cuts on a folded piece of paper produces the most amazing results. Such diverse things as a napkin ring, a mobile, notecards and a large wall decoration are all made with this method.

You will need:

A strip of thin coloured card or stiff paper 5cm by 20 cm (2in by 8in)
Scissors, glue

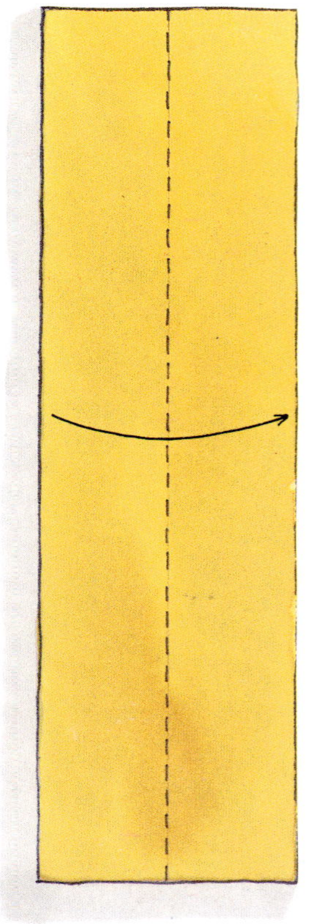

1 Fold the card in half lengthwise.

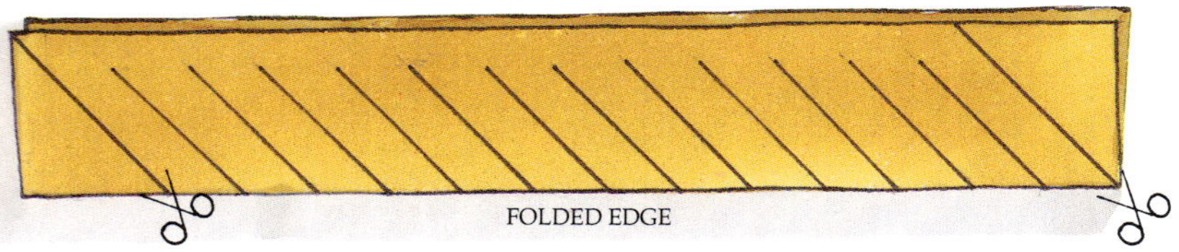

2 Cut parallel slits at an angle up to ½cm (¼in) of the long edge.

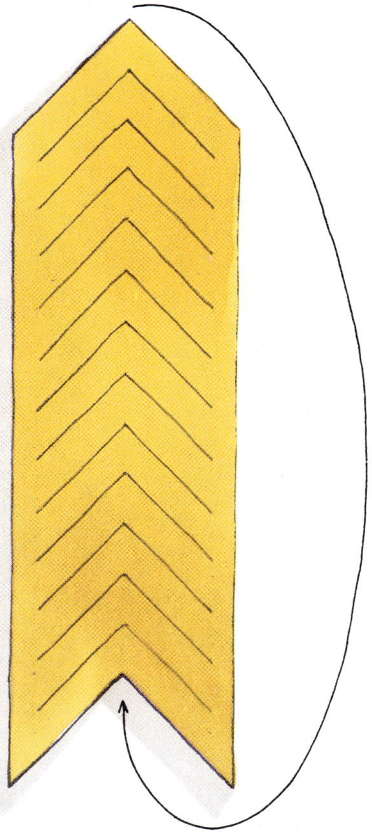

3 Unfold the card. Bend the short ends round to form a ring. Glue them together.

4 Bend back every other point to achieve a slightly different effect.

Variations

Cut the slits closer or wider to achieve different effects. Experiment by folding back different ribs. Shiny card gives especially attractive results.

Stand-Up Napkin

You can add splashes of colour to a dinner table by placing napkin rings with their circular openings up and setting a pleated napkin inside. For each place setting, pleat a napkin as follows.

You will need:

Paper or fabric napkin
Napkin ring as made on page 36

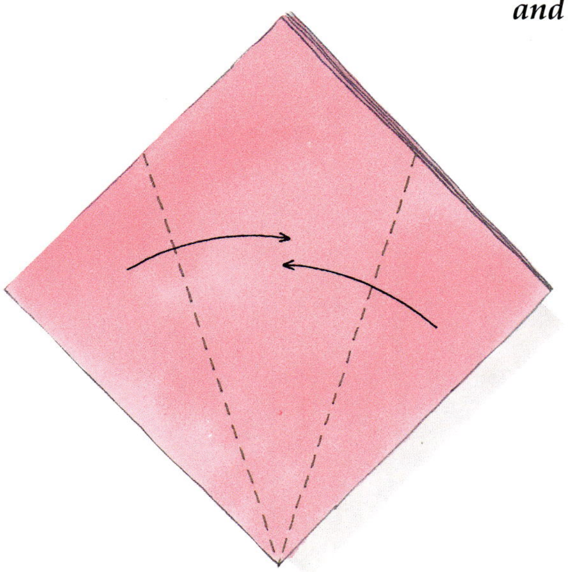

1 Begin with the napkin folded in quarters.

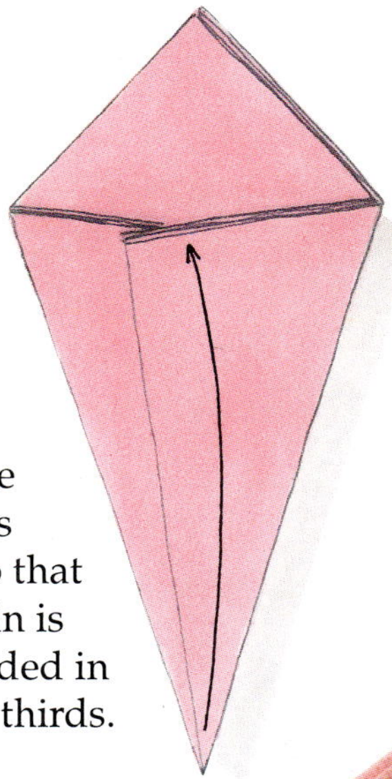

2 Fold in the corners as shown so that the napkin is folded in thirds.

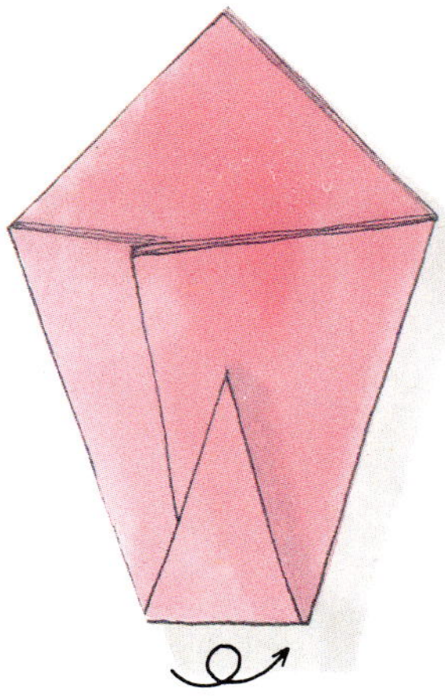

3 Fold up the bottom half. Turn the napkin back to front and place it into the napkin ring.

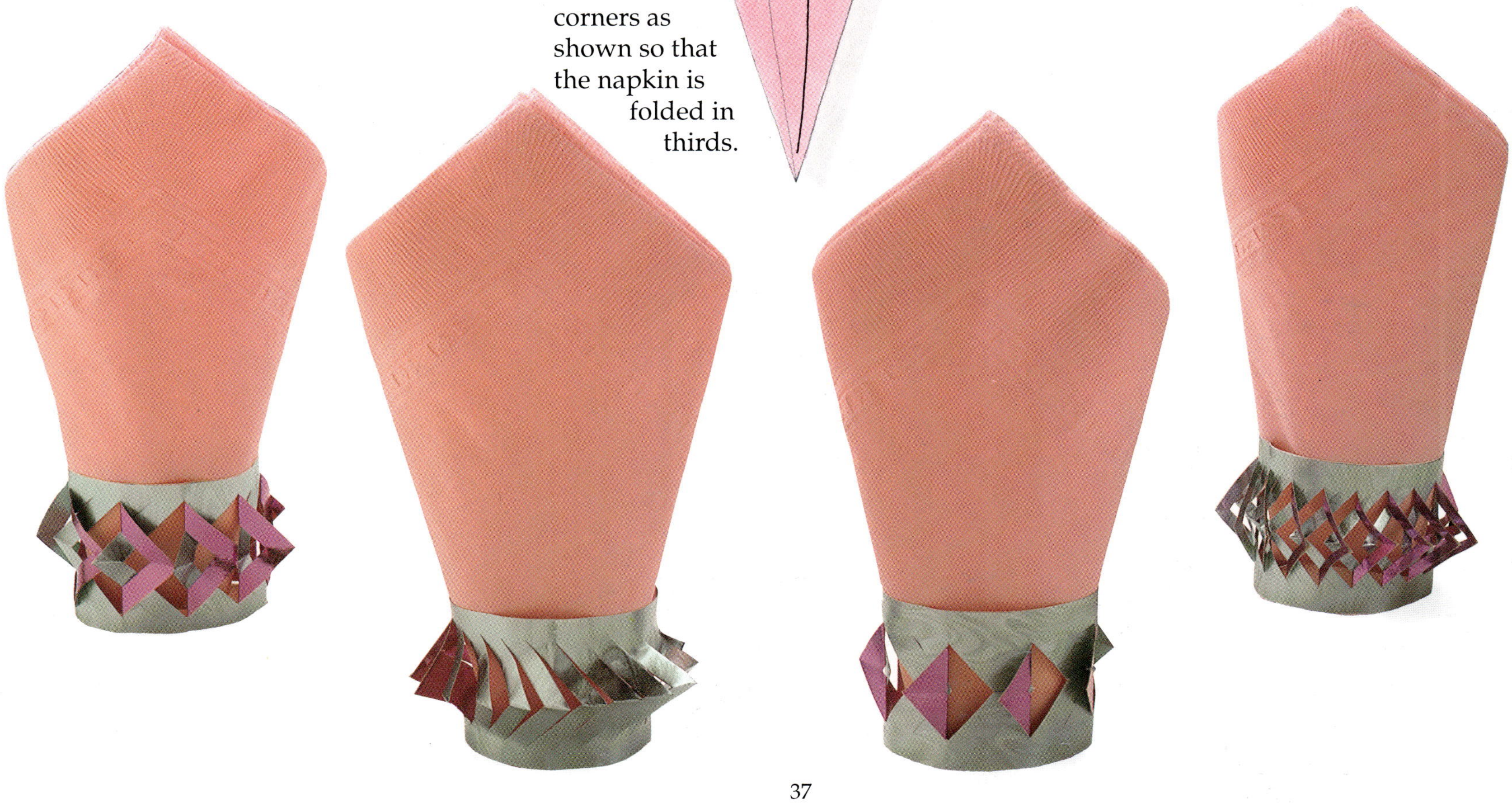

Mobile

One, two or more napkin rings can be made into a mobile. Hung out of reach from a lamp shade, the points and hollows will cast interesting shadows.

You will need:

Shiny coloured card in one or more colours
Thread
Scissors, glue

1 Make one, two, or more napkin rings as shown on page 36.

2 Knot a piece of thread to opposite sides of each ring.

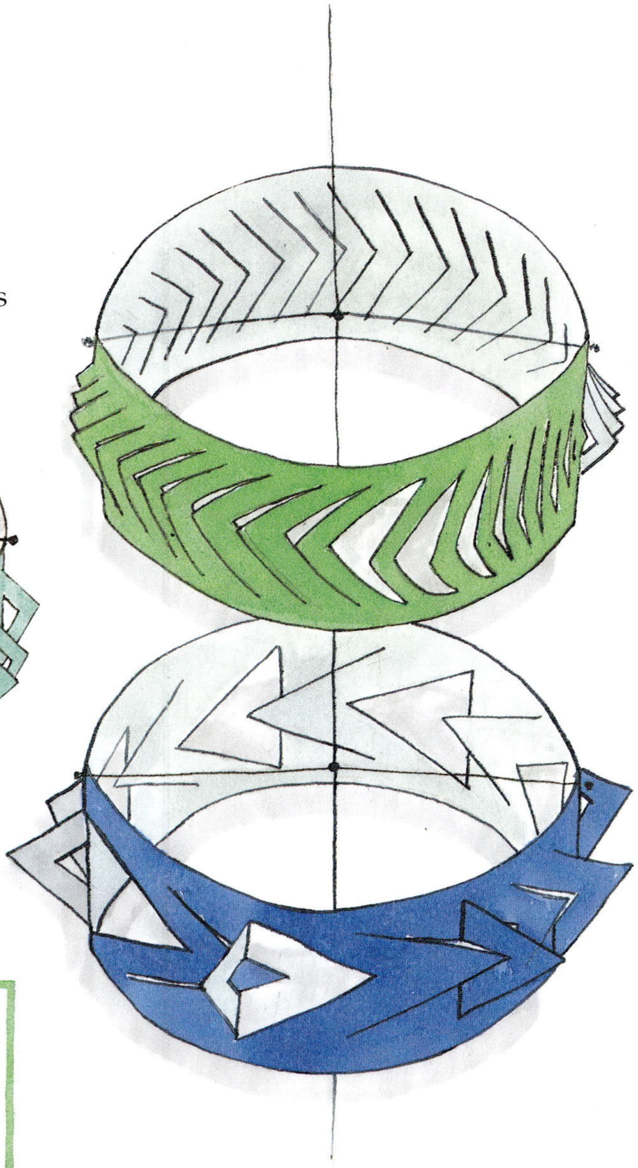

Variation

Make larger and smaller rings. Experiment by joining them in different ways.

3 Tie another piece of thread to the middle of the cross-thread on one ring. Then, leaving about 12cm (5in) of space on the thread, tie it to the cross-thread of the next ring, and so on, until all the rings are joined and you are ready to suspend the mobile.

Wall Hanging

The same parallel-cutting and folding can be used to make a spectacular wall hanging. Use paper which is coloured differently on each side or glue two pieces of different coloured paper together.

You will need

A long, large piece of duo-coloured paper, at least 13cm by 40cm (5in by 15in)
Thin card for backing 16cm by 43cm (7in by 17in)
Scissors

1 Follow the directions for the napkin ring (page 36), but leave flat after cutting the slits. Note the first and last cuts are not cut all the way to the opposite edge.

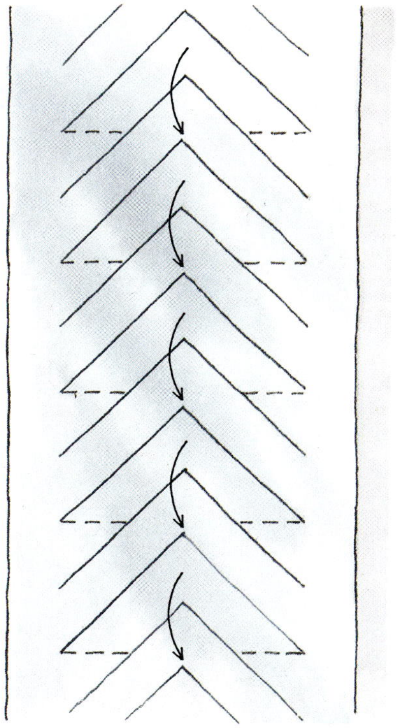

2 Fold down every other rib of paper.

3 Glue the paper onto the card.

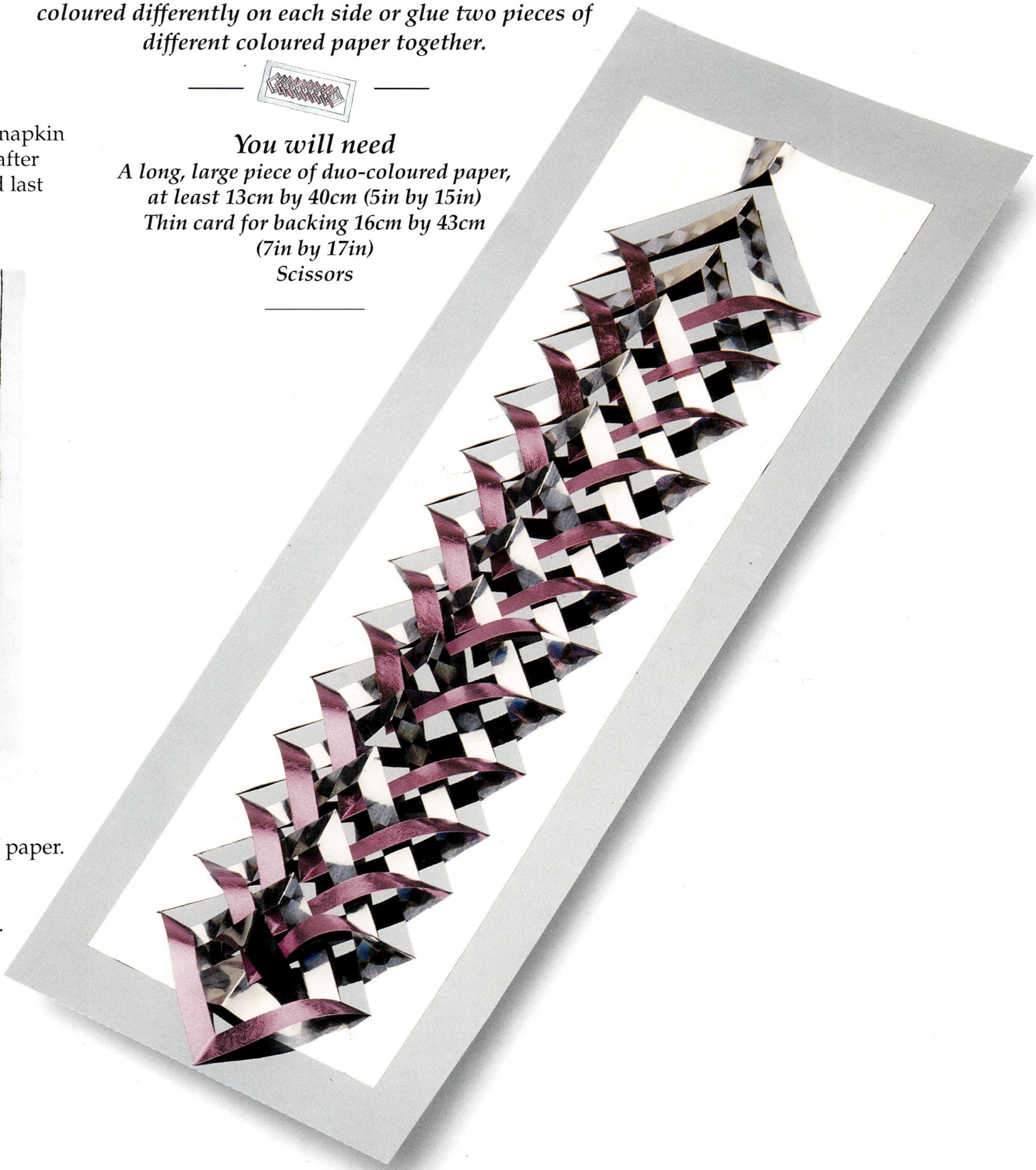

Parallel-Cut Notecards

You can decorate stationery with parallel-cut paper to create distinctive notecards. The design may look very complex, but once you have followed the directions you will find that it is really quite simple.

1 Cut a piece of coloured paper 4cm by 11cm (1½in by 4in).

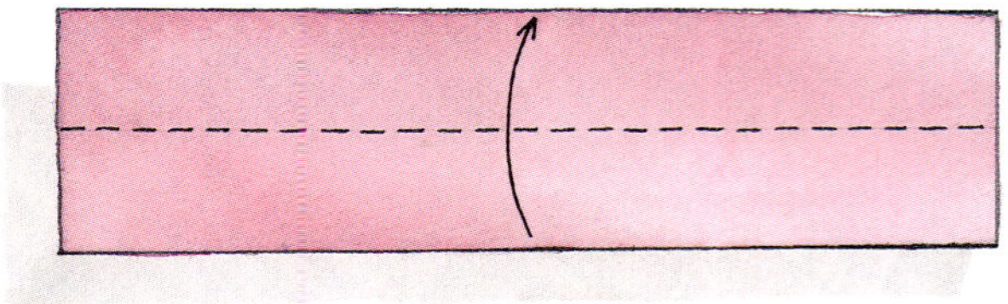

2 Fold this coloured paper in half.

You will need:

Blank card or notepaper 12cm by 15cm (4½in by 6in)
Paper in two colours
Ruler, pencil, scissors, glue

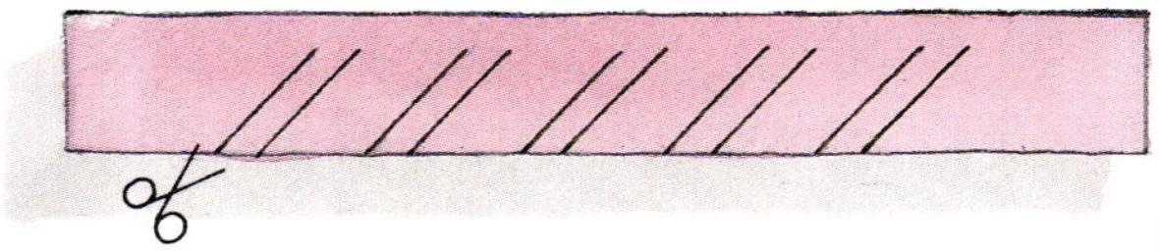

3 Cut five pairs of parallel slits at an angle, beginning at the folded edge and ending ½cm (¼in) away from the raw edges. Unfold the paper.

4 Fold up every other point.

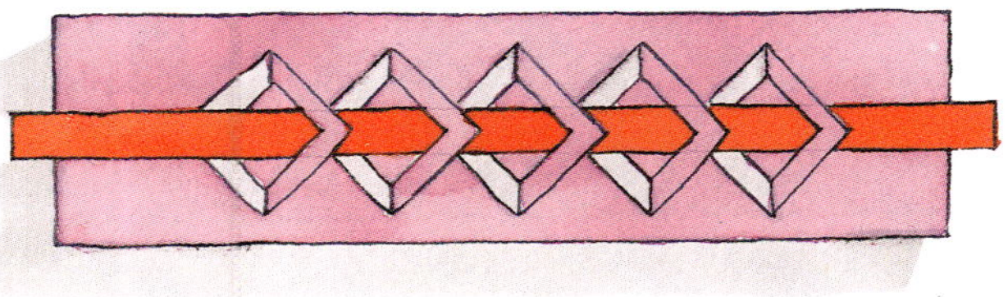

5 Cut a narrow strip of paper 1cm (½in) wide and 14cm (5½in) long. Slide it under the bent-up sections.

6 Glue the design to the front of the blank card.

Christmas Tree Card

Simple parallel-cutting can help you make many Christmas cards in a very short time. All members of the family can take part in the fun and perhaps add their own ideas for extra decorations.

You will need:

Blank red card 13cm by 18cm (5in by 7in)
Green foil giftwrap
2cm (¾in) gold star sticker
Ruler, pencil, scissors, glue

1 Cut a piece of green paper 8cm by 12cm (3in by 4¾in).

2 Fold the paper in half.

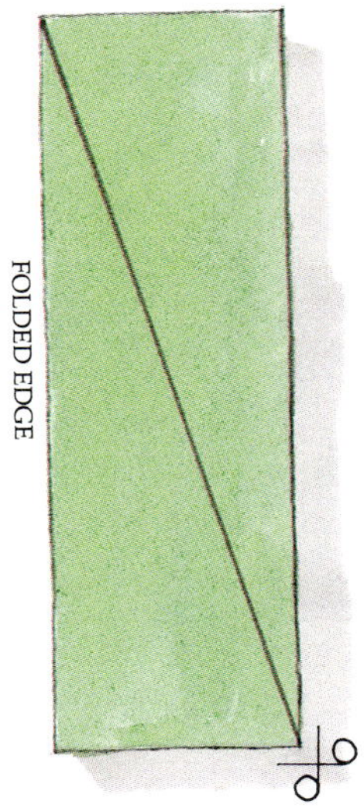

3 Draw a pencil line from corner to corner. Cut on the line through both layers of paper.

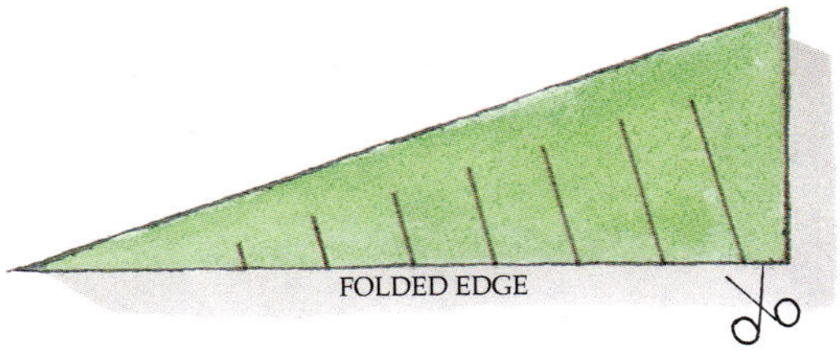

4 Cut parallel slits at an angle, beginning at the folded edge and ending about ½cm (¼in) away from the raw edges. Unfold the paper.

5 Fold up all the triangles.

6 Glue one, two or three green trees on the red card. Stick gold stars at the top of each.

It's a Bloom!

This is a very simple, yet dramatic, decoration, for which you can find many uses. For a wedding large white blooms can be suspended from the ceiling and smaller ones set in every glass on the festive table. Pastel-shaded blooms are good for Easter and red, green and gold ones for Christmas.

You will need:

A sheet of A4 paper, white or coloured
Scissors, pencil, stapler or glue, ruler

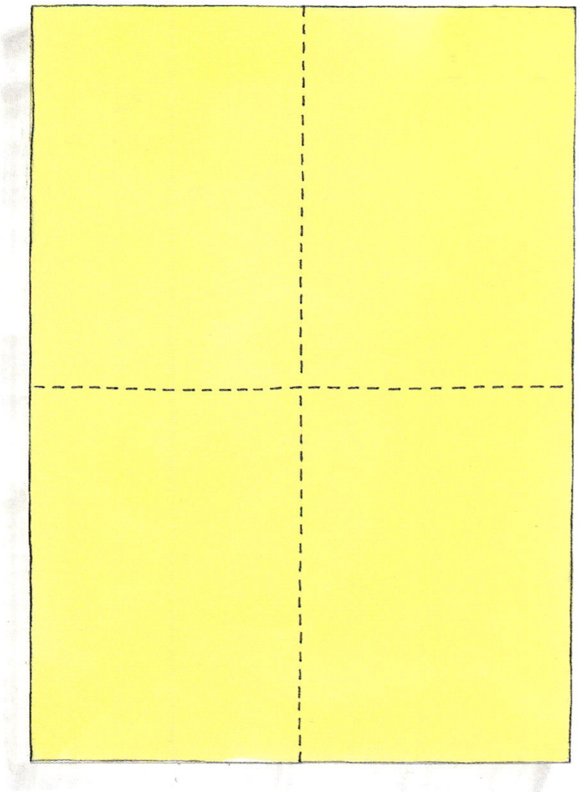

1 Fold the paper in quarters.

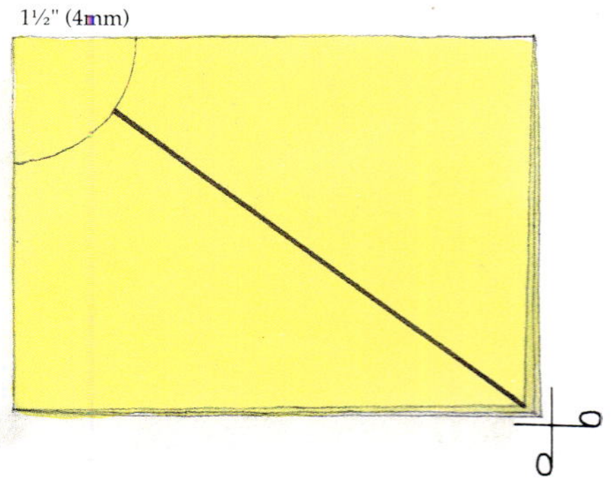

2 Draw a curve 4cm (1½in) from the closed corner, which is the middle of the paper. Draw in the diagonal starting opposite the closed corner and stopping at the curve, as shown.

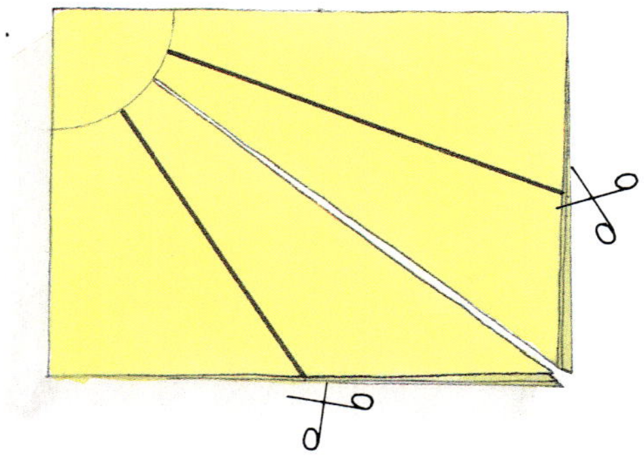

3 Mark the midpoints of the open sides and draw a line to the closed corner, stopping at the curve. Cut along the lines, stopping at the curve. Unfold the paper.

4 Cut along the four creases, stopping 4cm (1½in) from the middle. Number the corners as shown, in pencil.

5 Bring together corners with the same number and staple or glue them in place, that is: Bring the four number 1 corners together, and staple them.

Variations

Combine the corners in other ways.

Wedding Blooms

This time use white paper about 15cm by 21cm (6in by 8½in).

Mobile

Make a larger bloom from a larger sheet of paper and suspend it by a thread tied or glued to the top staple.

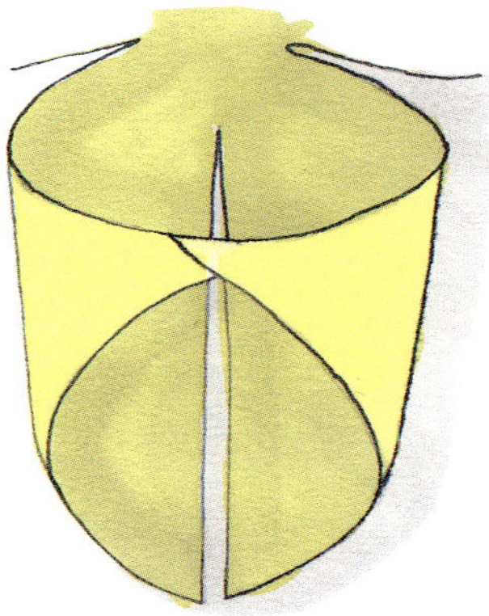

6 Staple together the two corners numbered 2.
Staple together the two corners numbered 3.
Staple together the two corners numbered 4, overlapping them exactly.
Staple together the two corners numbered 5, overlapping them exactly.
Bring together underneath the four corners numbered 6 and staple them.

Jack's Beanstalk

This is an old trick often used by magicians. It can be performed by anyone after practising it a few times.

You will need:

4 large sheets of newspaper
Sticky tape or glue, scissors

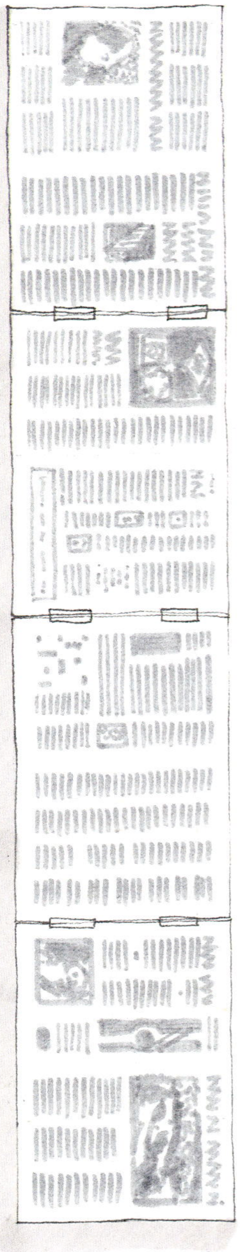

1 Lay the sheets of newspaper side by side and stick the shorter sides together, as shown.

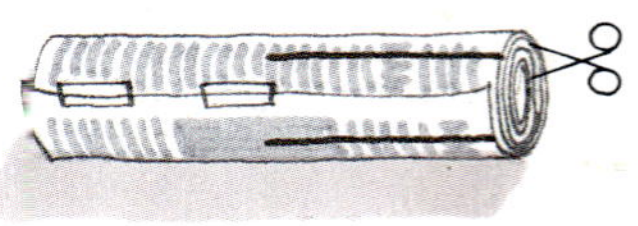

2 Roll the paper up loosely, leaving an inner space about as thick as your thumb. The outside diameter of the completed roll should be about 4 to 5 cm (1½ to 2in). Glue or tape one end and the middle of the roll.

3 Make a vertical cut to halfway down the side of the roll. Make two more cuts evenly spaced round the roll.

4 Reach inside the roll and slowly pull up and extend the paper into a 1¼metre (4ft) tree.

Party Magic

Perform the trick as party entertainment for small children. Give older children newspaper to try the trick themselves.

Tree Decoration

You can also spray paint the trees and stick them into pots.

Leatherlike Gift Box

The unusual leatherlike look on this handsome gift box is achieved by covering it with masking tape and brown shoe polish. Other colours, such as red and black, produce a mosaic look.

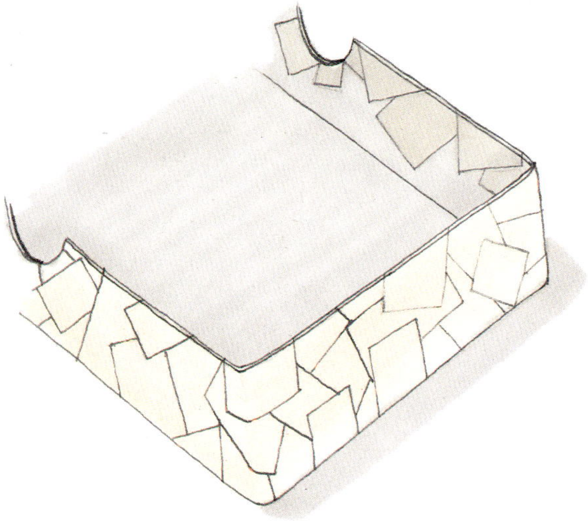

You will need:

A box to cover, about 15cm by 10cm (6in by 4in)
Brown shoe polish (solid)
Masking tape, 2cm (⅞in or ½in) wide
Scissors, glue, paper towels

Caution: Shoe polish stains clothing and furnishings. Children should always be closely supervised by an adult.

Larger Boxes

Decorate larger boxes with wider masking tape.

Other Objects

Apply the leatherlike finish to frames and other things.

1 Cut masking tape into approximately 3cm (1½in) pieces as you proceed. Cover the lid, including the sides, overlapping the strips at random. Tuck the ends inside the lid.

2 With paper towels, rub the shoe polish all over the lid. It will look brown with darker brown lines where the polish accumulates against the edges of the masking tape.

3 Spread glue all over with a small piece of sponge or brush. Let the box dry completely, until the glue is transparent and no longer sticky to the touch. Spread a second coating of glue and let it dry.

Lamb Chop Cuffs

You have probably seen paper cuffs on lamb chops in restaurants and fancy food magazines. Perhaps you have wondered how they are made. You may be surprised how simple it is not only to add them to lamb chops but to use them as decorations on food platters. In a large size they look like pom-poms and turn out to be even more versatile.

You will need:

White or pastel-coloured paper
Scissors, glue

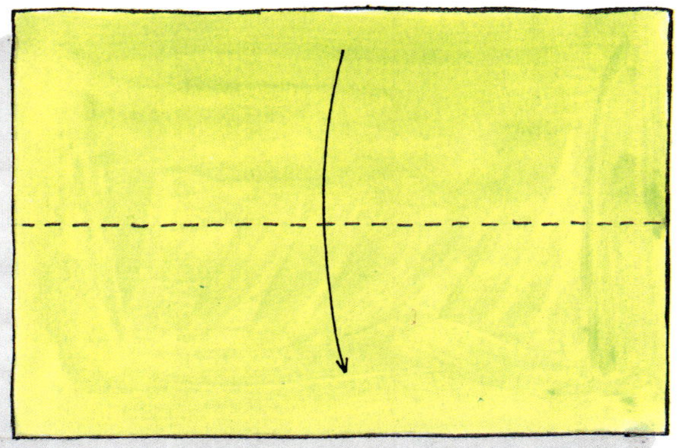

1 Cut the paper into a rectangle 15cm by 10cm (6in by 4in). Fold it in half lengthwise.

2 Cut slits from the folded edge, about 2cm (¾in) deep, the closer together the better.

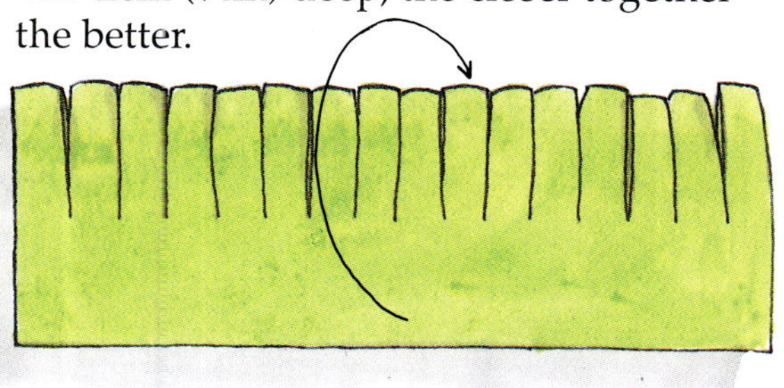

3 Bring the front layer of the paper to the back. This eliminates the sharp crease and makes the cuff fluffy.

4 Roll paper around your little finger or a pen. Glue the end.

Variations

Make bigger cuffs for turkey legs from a piece of paper 25cm by 15cm (10in by 6in).

For a gift package decoration, use tissue paper 35cm by 20cm (15in by 8in).

Large tissue paper cuffs can be turned into pom-poms. Insert a dowel stick into the middle and drip in some glue. Squeeze the bottom of the cuff close to the dowel stick.

Decoupaged Eggs

The word 'decoupage' may sound mysterious but comes from the French word 'coupage' which means cutting. Decoupage was originally used on furniture. Illustrations were pasted on to make it appear hand-painted. This process can also be used to decorate Easter eggs with patterns cut from paper napkins.

You will need

A hard boiled egg
Patterned paper napkins
A small piece of sponge
PVC (white) glue, scissors

Caution: Do not eat the eggs after they have been decoupaged.

1 With the sponge wipe glue all over the egg. First cover the front and leave it for about ten minutes until it is no longer milky and sticky, but clear and dry. Turn the egg over and cover the back with glue.

2 While the egg is drying, cut out designs from the paper napkin. You can leave a white margin around the design if it is very intricate - it will disappear in the glue. Separate the patterned layer from the backing layer.

3 Wipe another coating of glue onto the front of the egg. Carefully pat on the cutouts at once and let the egg dry again. Turn the egg over and repeat on the back.

4 Wipe on a final coat of glue.

Coloured Eggs

You can colour the eggs all over before decoupaging them. Choose colours that complement the napkin cutouts.

Plastic Eggs

Styrofoam and other eggs can be decoupaged in the same way as hard-boiled eggs.

Woven Basket

This basket is quite mysterious. By interweaving two pieces of paper you end up with a basket which you fill with little surprises. Use it for party decorations or hang it on the Christmas tree, as is customary in Denmark.

You will need:
Red and white paper
Scissors, glue

> ## *Party Time*
> *Older children can make their own baskets. Use larger strips for bigger baskets to take home party goodies.*

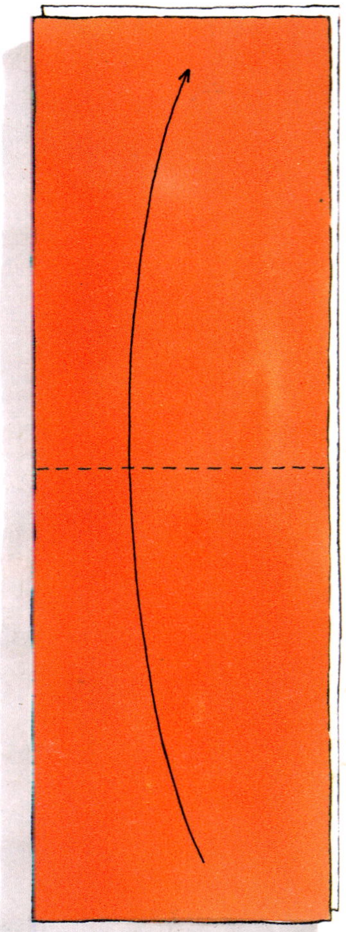

1 From each sheet of coloured paper cut a piece 10cm by 30cm (4in by 12in). Fold each piece in half the short way.

2 Beginning at the folded edge cut 2½cm (1in) strips, ending about 2½cm (1in) away from the opposite end.

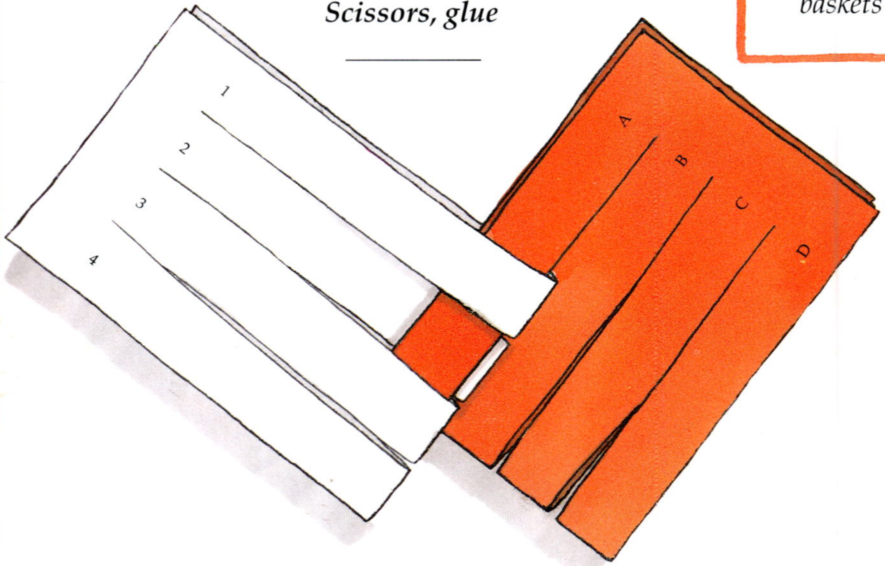

3 Place strip A between the layers of strip 1. Place strip 2 between the layers of strip A. Continue weaving by repeating these two motions.

4 Push strip A up and then weave strip B by first placing strip 1 between the layers of strip B. Then place strip B between the layers of strip 2 and so on.

5 Weave strip C as you did strip A and weave strip D as you did strip B. Cut scallops at the top edges.

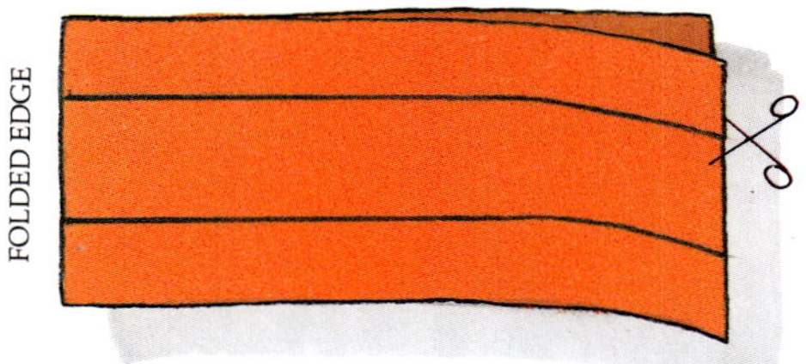

6 From each colour cut a piece 5cm by 30cm (2in by 12in). Cut out curved handles from both as shown.

7 Glue the handles to the inside of the basket.

Four-Pointed Star

Stars are very popular decorations, but you may not know that it is easy to produce symmetrical stars with only one cut, after the paper has been folded in different ways shown in the next four pages. You can use stars on gift packages, stationery, mobiles and as Christmas ornaments. Giftwrap and origami paper give the most colourful results, with foil giftwrap a clear favourite.

You will need:
A piece of paper
Scissors

1 Fold the paper into quarters.

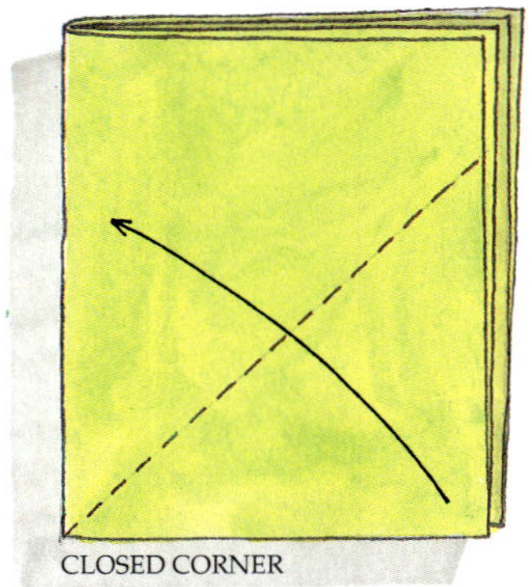

2 Look for the closed corner, which is the centre of the paper. Fold this corner in half.

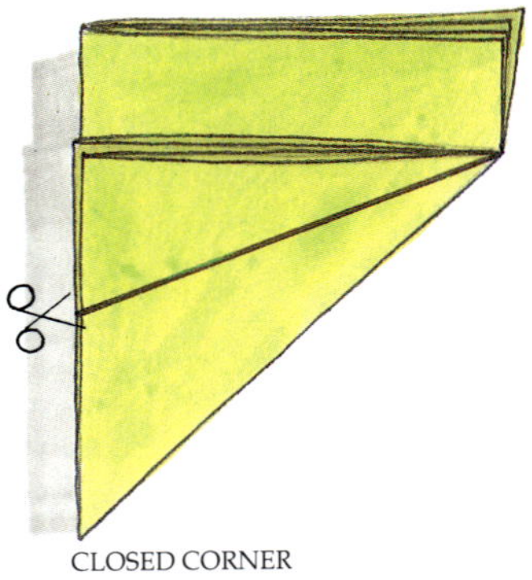

3 Make a slanted cut through all the layers as shown.

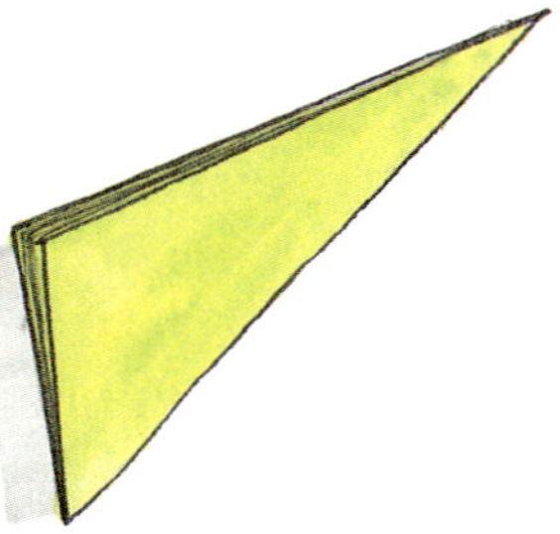

4 Your paper now looks like this and is ready to be unfolded into a four-pointed star.

Change the Angles

The angle of the points can be very shallow or very spiky. It only depends on the angle at which you make the one important cut.

Eight-Pointed Star

This is made very much like the four-pointed star, but the paper is folded in half again before cutting.

You will need:
A piece of paper
Scissors

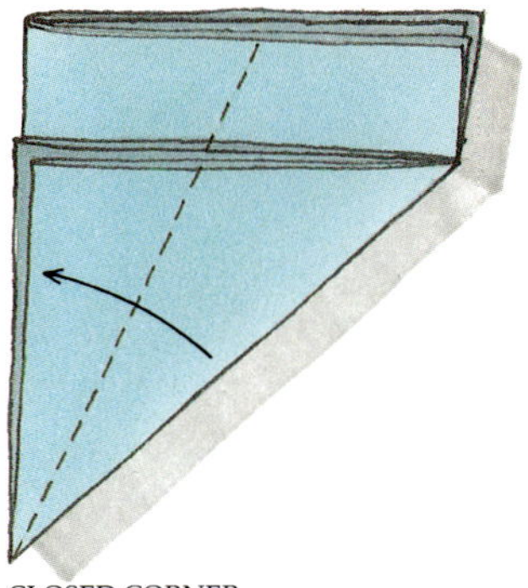

CLOSED CORNER

1 Fold steps 1 and 2 of the four-pointed star. Fold the closed corner in half once more.

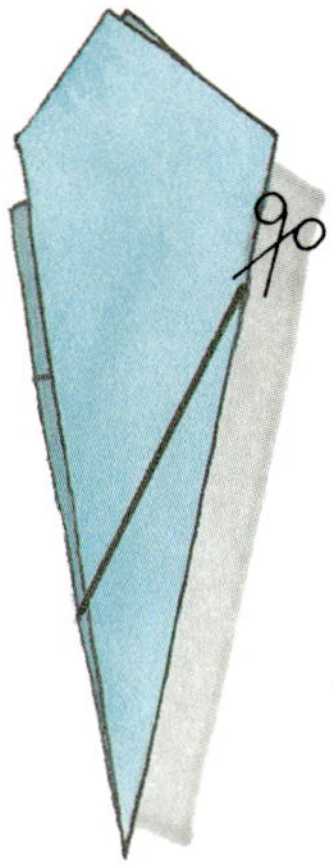

2 Cut from the corner shown at a sharp angle to the opposite edge.

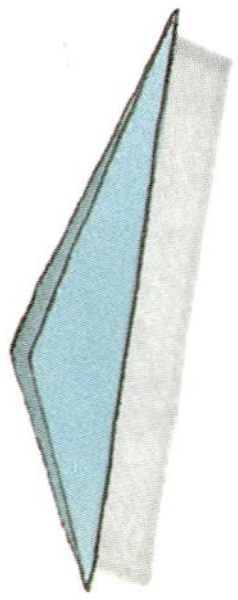

3 Your paper now looks like this and is ready to be unfolded.

Stars from Card

If you would like to make stars from heavy paper or card, you may find that is is too heavy to be folded. In that case cut a star from lighter-weight paper and use it as a pattern. Place it on top of the card and trace around it. Then cut around the outline.

Five-Pointed Star

You will not have any difficulty in cutting five-pointed stars if you always begin with a piece of paper in the proportion of 4 by 5.

You will need:
A piece of paper 20cm by 25cm
(8in by 10in)
Pencil, scissors

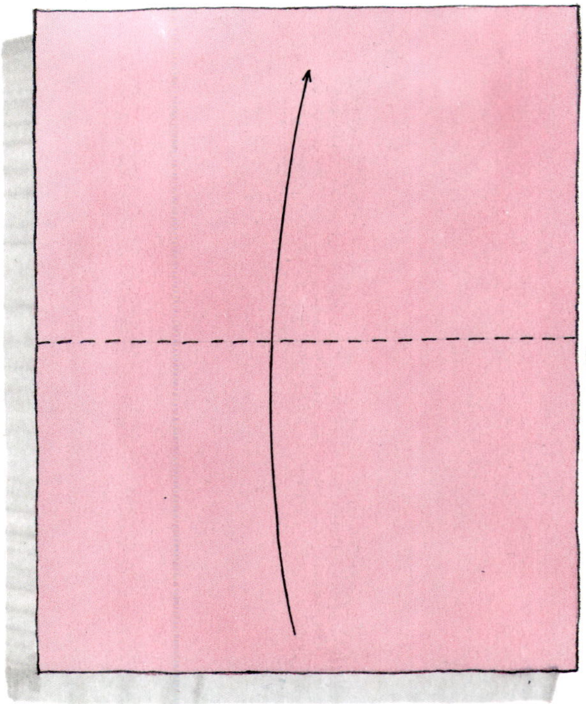

1 Fold in half by placing the short sides together.

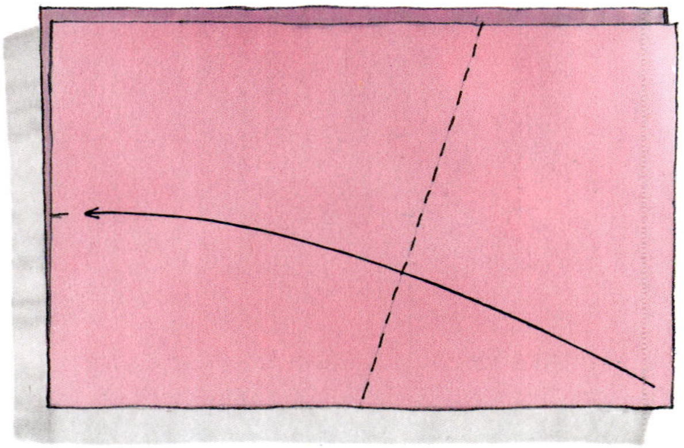

2 Mark the middle of the short left edge lightly with pencil. Bring the right-hand corner to the mark on the opposite edge and crease as shown.

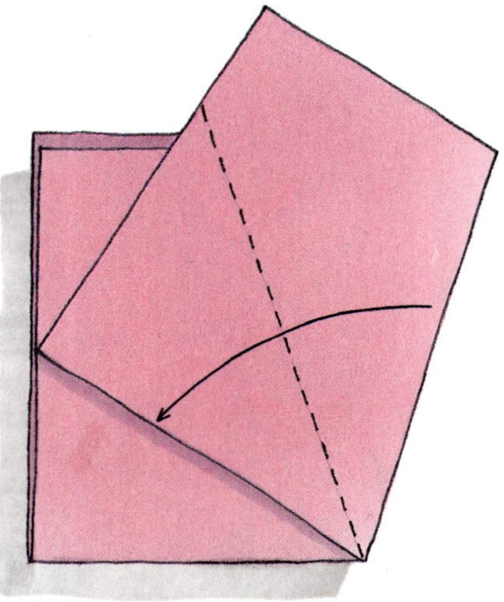

3 Fold the right-hand edge over to the left and crease as shown.

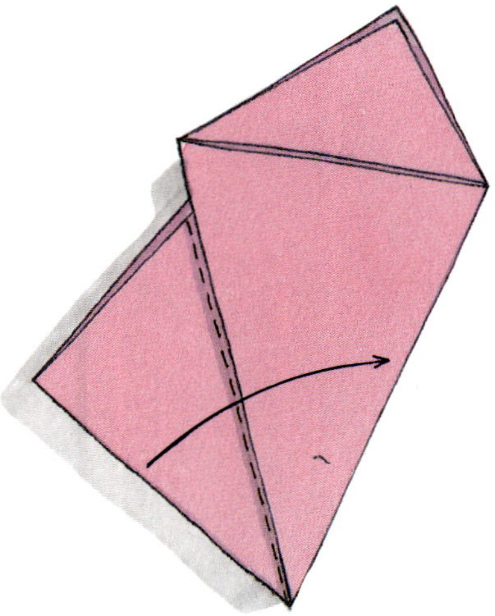

4 Fold the left edge over to the right and crease as shown.

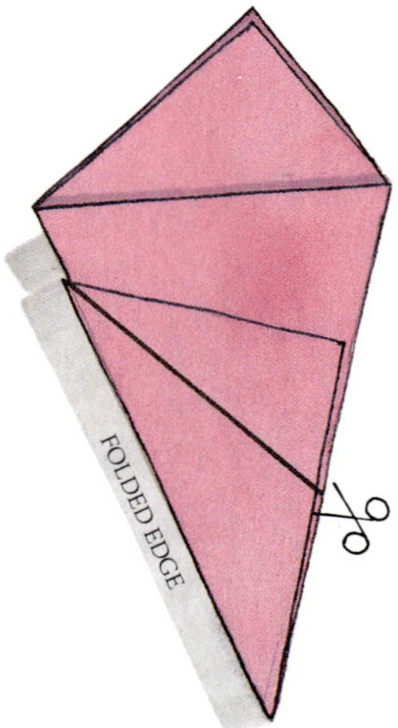

5 Cut at the angle shown.

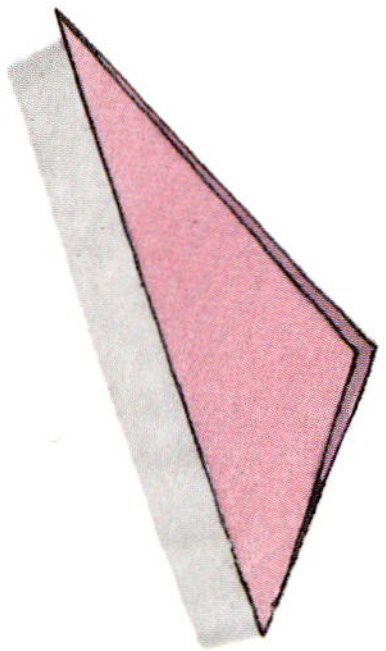

6 The paper now looks like this and is then ready to be unfolded.

Six-Pointed Star

This is made in much the same way as the other stars, but the paper is folded in a different way.

You will need:
A square of paper
Scissors

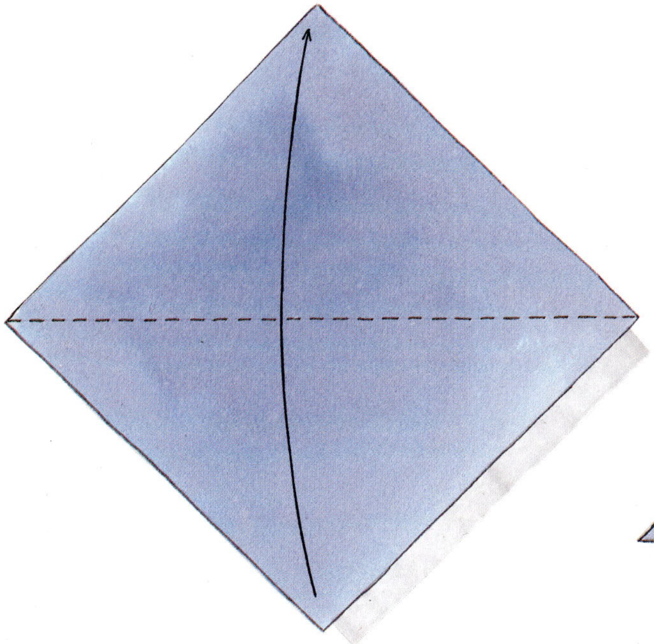

1 Fold the paper on the diagonal.

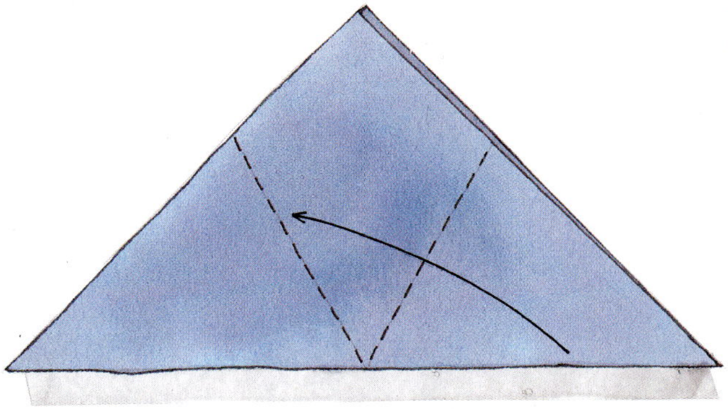

2 Lightly mark the middle of the folded edge.

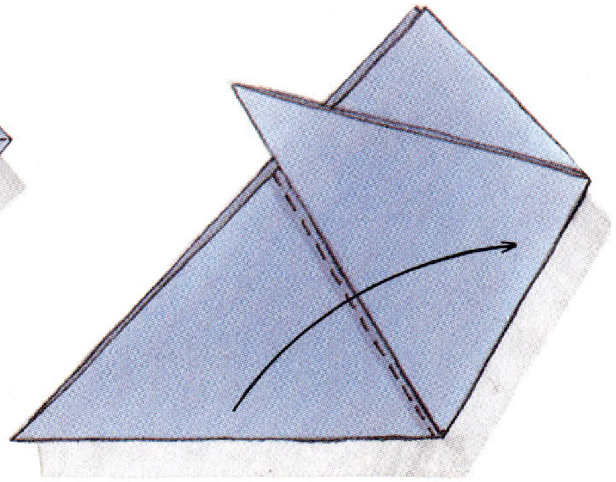

3 Fold the paper into equal thirds by folding the right corner to the left, then the left corner to the right from the middle point. Slide the paper until the edges align.

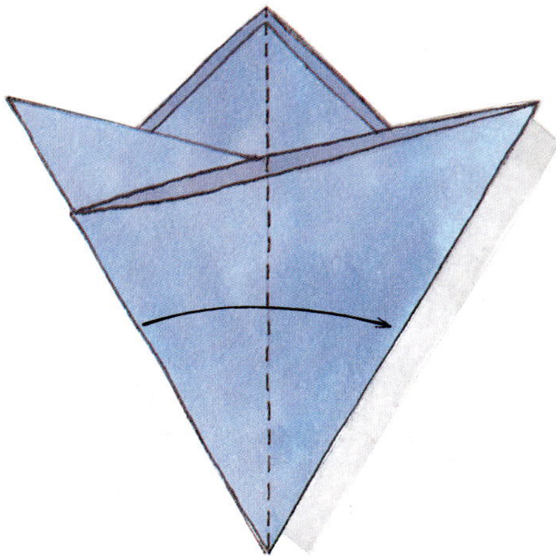

4 Fold the paper in half.

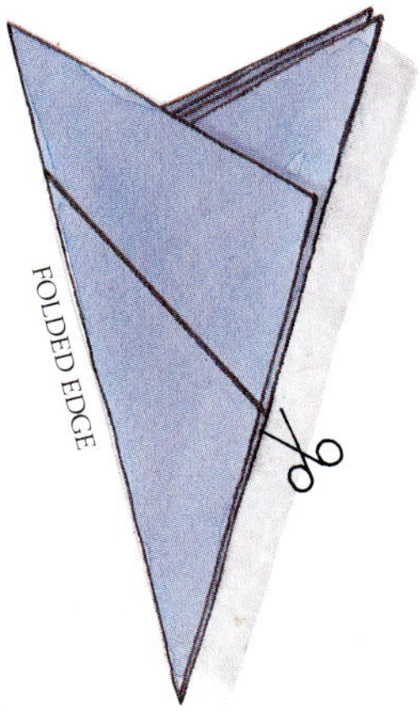

5 Cut at an angle as shown.

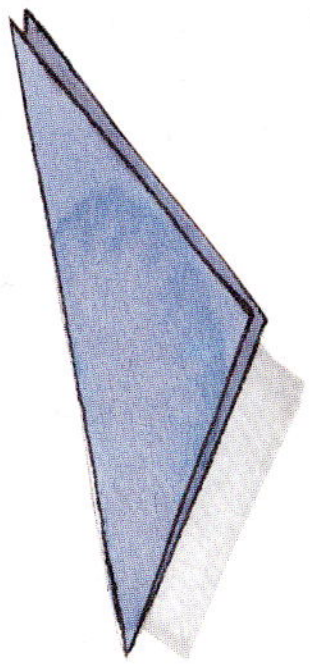

6 The paper now looks like this. Before unfolding, the centre can be cut out as shown on page 55. Unfold.

Star Variations

Now that you know how to cut various stars, you can have fun making them more interesting. Cut away areas for a lacy appearance. Cut curves instead of straight lines. Layer small stars on top of larger ones. The examples shown here are just a few of the possibilities. The ideas are interchangable: if layering is shown with an eight-pointed star, why not try it with a five-pointed star. Take a few pieces of paper and just experiment. You may be surprised at the many pleasing designs that appear.

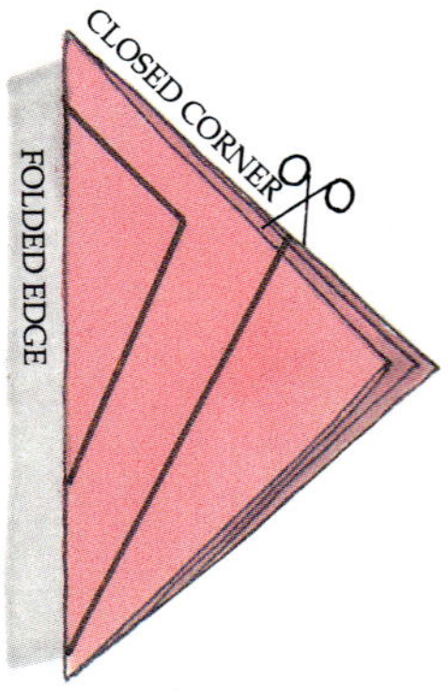

Lacy Stars

The first lacy star is made from a four-pointed star. Follow instructions 1 to 4 but make the additional cuts before unfolding the star.

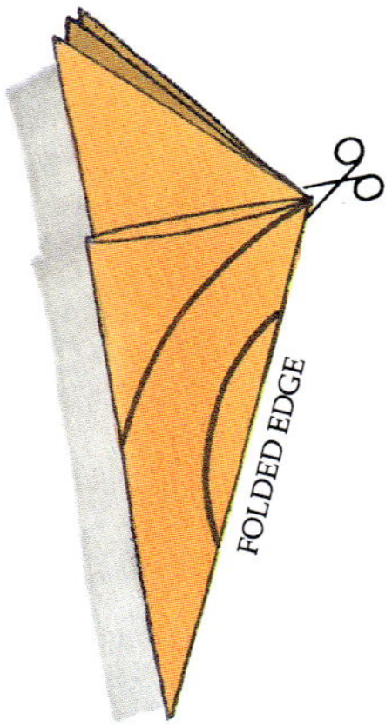

The second lacy star is made from the eight-pointed star. Follow instructions 1 to 3 and make the additional cuts before unfolding the star.

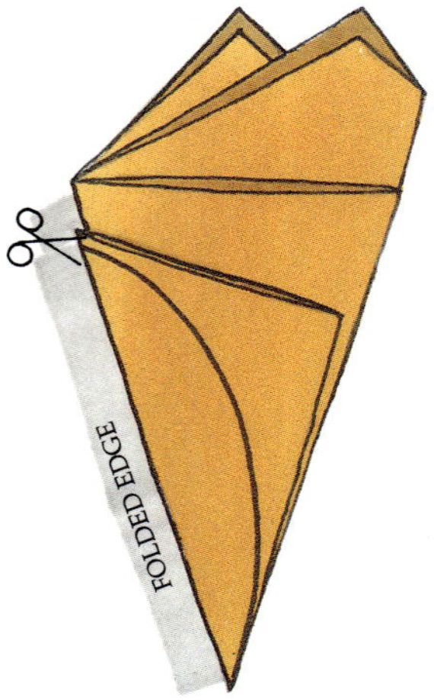

Flower

Fold the five-pointed star and cut as shown before unfolding.

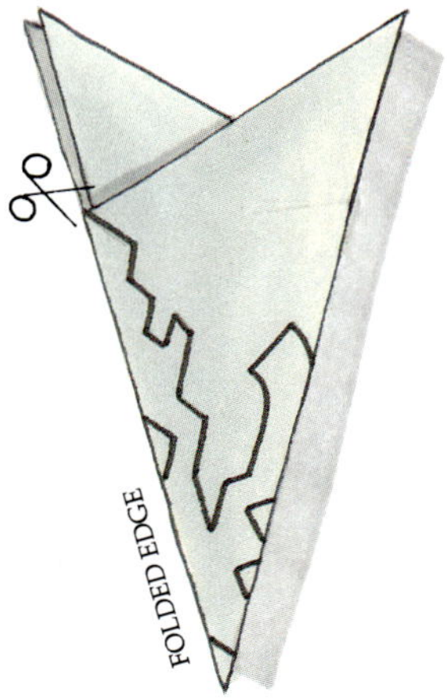

Snowflake
Fold the six-pointed star then cut any pattern you like into the folded edges. Be sure not to cut all the way across to the other folded edge so that your snowflake holds together.

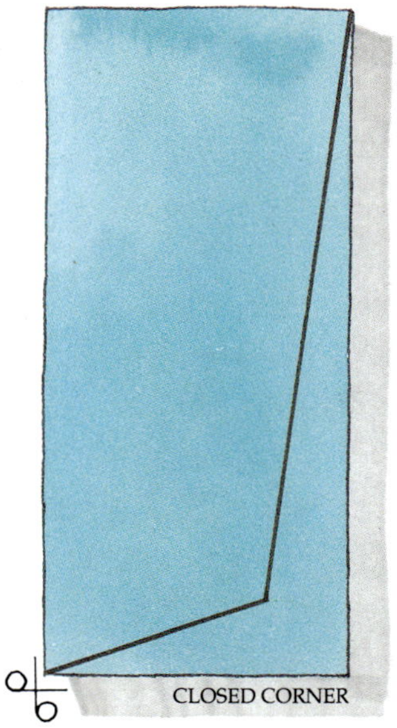

Star of Bethlehem
Use a rectangular piece of paper. Fold it into quarters. Make two angled cuts as shown.

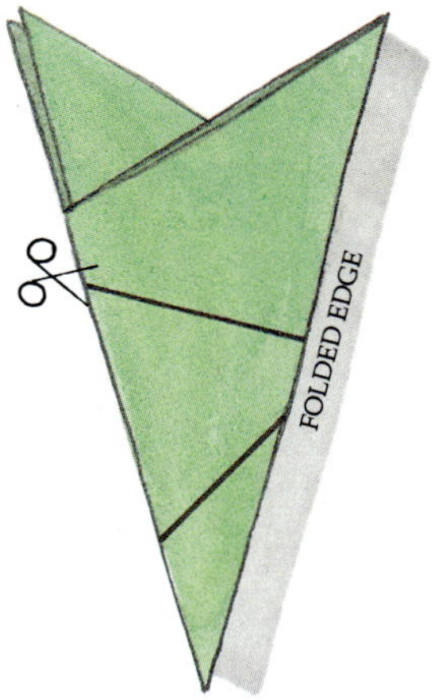

Hexagon
Fold as for the six-pointed star and cut as shown.

Star Garland
Make several six-pointed stars and Stars of David. Stretch a string across the area where you want to hang the garland. Attach the stars over the string with sticky tape. Alternate the two kinds of stars. You may find it easier to attach the stars to the string by stretching it between two chairs. When complete, fix the garland up high.

Hanging Star
This four-pointed star was decorated with parallel cuts, as shown on page 36. The cuts are done before the paper is unfolded. The points are gathered and glued together. The star is then ready to be suspended.

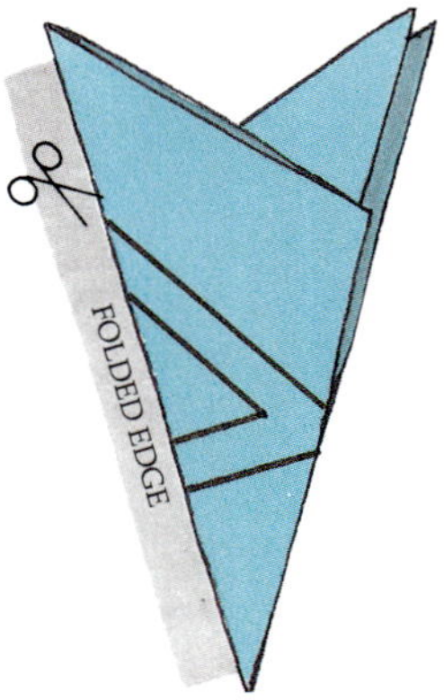

Star of David
Fold as for the six-pointed star and cut as shown. An alternative way of cutting the centre is also shown.

Three-Dimensional Stars

You can make any star three-dimensional. Crease up mountain folds through all the long points and crease down valley folds in between. You can make stars from card three-dimensional by scoring on opposite sides of the card instead of making mountain and valley folds. For scoring see page 13.

Origami

Origami is the art of folding paper, without any cutting or gluing, into anything, whether animal, mineral, vegetable, realistic or fantastic. In this section you will find step-by-step instructions for making animals, greetings cards, table decorations and other things. The words 'paperfolding' and 'origami' are inter-changeable, both meaning the same but in English and Japanese. The art is most popular in Japan and has travelled from there to other parts of the world. Now people in many countries enjoy paperfolding as an engrossing hobby. They have added their own creations to those traditionally handed down from generation to generation, not only in Japan, but in their own countries.

Before you begin, be sure to look at the key to symbols on page 8. In addition I would like to mention that paperfolders use other special terms, some of which are introduced and explained in the instructions for the paper projects. For example, bases are a series of beginning steps which can lead to many different designs. See the kite base on page 66 and the bird base on page 82.

I hope you will enjoy these examples of origami for your own pleasure and to share with others.

Greetings Card

This greetings card is simple to do and looks quite attractive made only with wrapping paper, or you can make it with coloured paper and decorate it. It is the first in a sequence of origami projects, which all begin in exactly the same way and add a new step each time. They are shown on the next four pages.

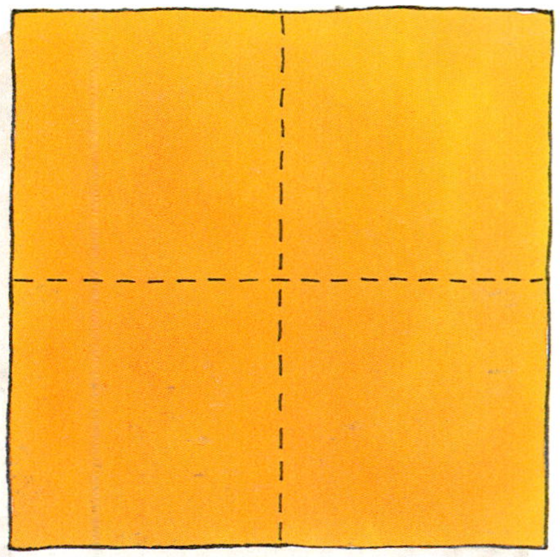

1 Fold the square in half. Unfold and fold in half the other way. Unfold.

You will need:

A 20cm (8in) square of coloured paper or giftwrap

2 Fold the four corners to the centre and write your message on the inside.

Surprise Card

You can decorate the inside, perhaps with a patchwork design (see page 20), or you can put a folded origami bird or other surprise inside it. You can send the card in an envelope or glue it closed with a sticker or paper cutout.

Tooth Fairy Pillow

The Tooth Fairy visits every time a child loses one of its first teeth, provided the tooth is hidden under the pillow at bedtime. In the morning the child wakes up eager to find out how much money the Tooth Fairy has left in exchange for the tooth. A Tooth Fairy pillow made from three layers of paper adds a charming note to the custom.

You will need:

Three paper squares of sides 20cm, 15cm and 10cm (8in, 6in and 4in)
A sticker or paper doily
Tooth Fairy money

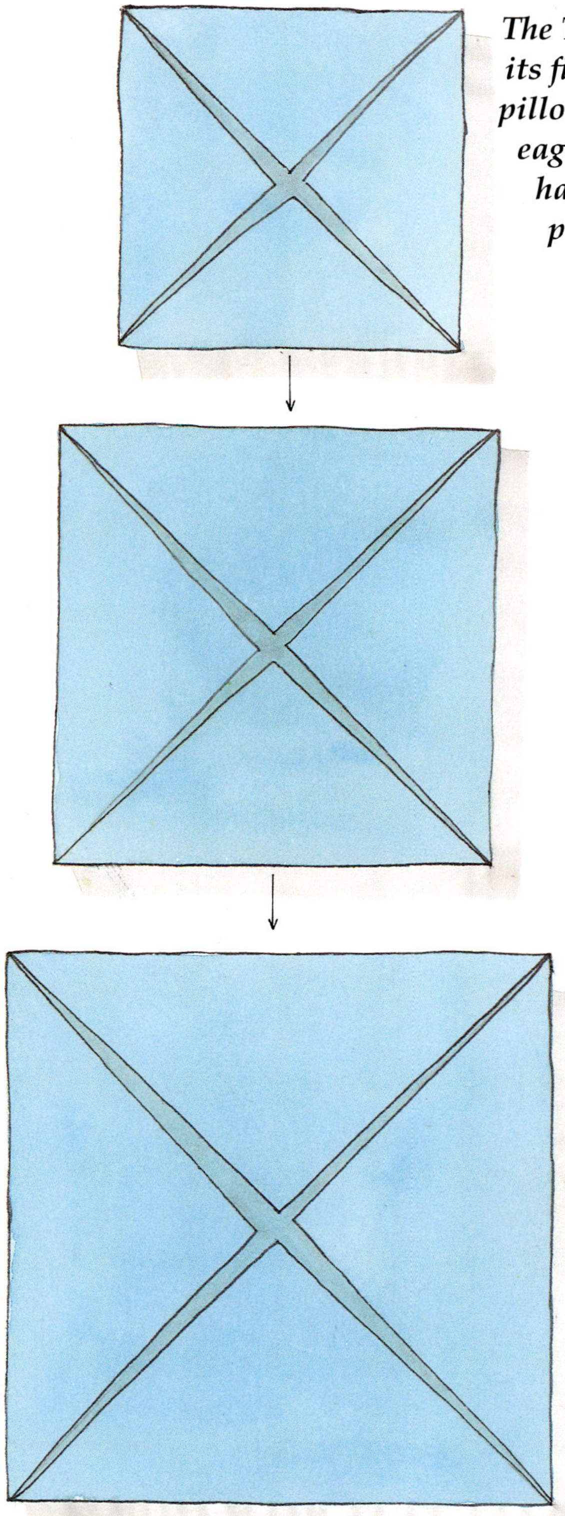

1 Fold all three squares like the greetings card.

2 Put the money inside the smallest card. Then insert it in the next larger card, and put both inside the largest card.

3 Seal the centre of the card with a sticker or part of a doily.

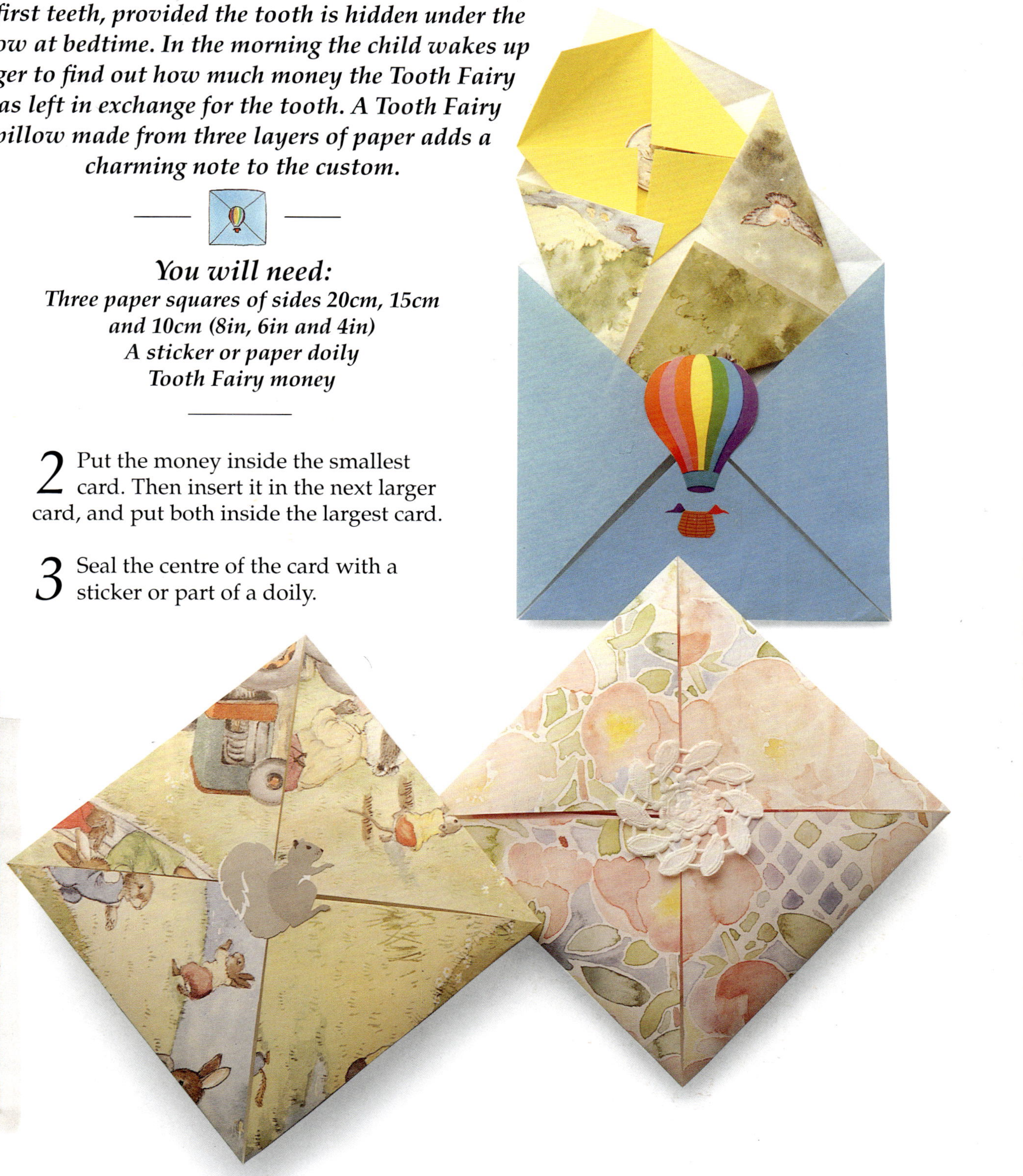

Petal Coaster

This coaster is a slight variation on the usual flat kind and serves a double purpose: it absorbs moisture from the glass and it looks pretty.

You will need:
A 20cm (8in) square piece of coloured paper or giftwrap

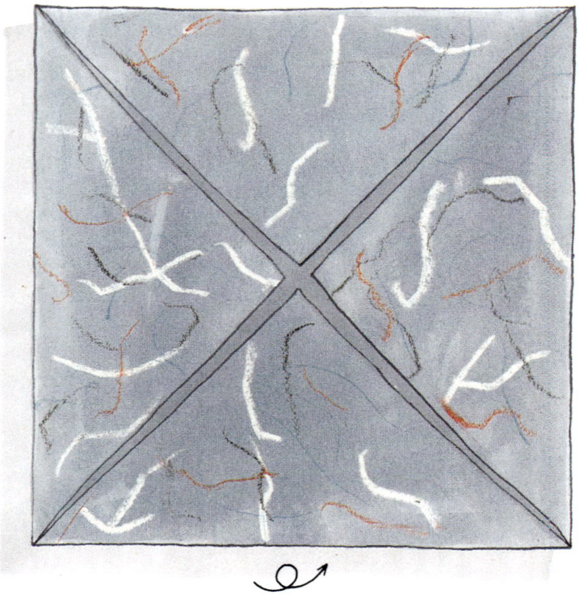

1 Fold the paper into the greetings card. Turn the paper over.

2 Fold the four corners to the centre.

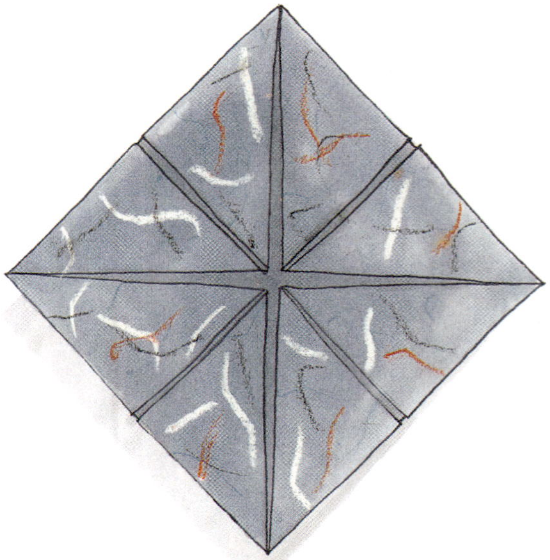

3 The coaster is complete and ready to have a glass placed on it.

Frame

Most pictures look much better when framed. This origami frame adds importance to any family photograph or other image and can be sent flat. It looks especially nice when made from giftwrap with a small pattern.

You will need:

A square of paper, with sides 20cm (8in) or twice as long as the square photo you want to frame

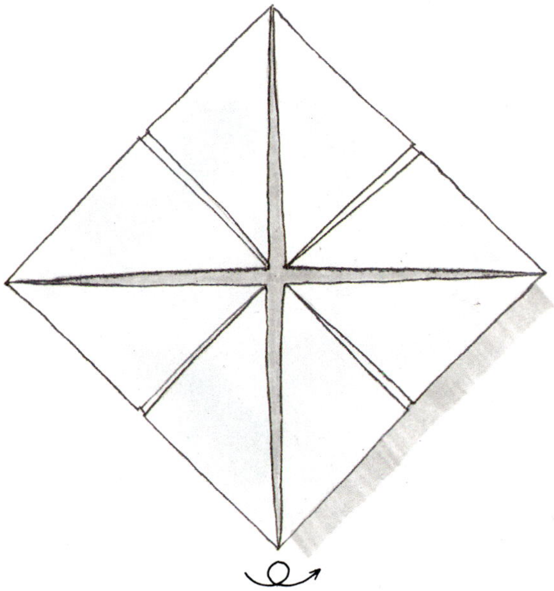

1 If the paper is coloured on one side only, begin with the coloured side up. Fold the coaster. Turn it over from back to front.

2 Fold the four corners *from* the centre to the outside edges.

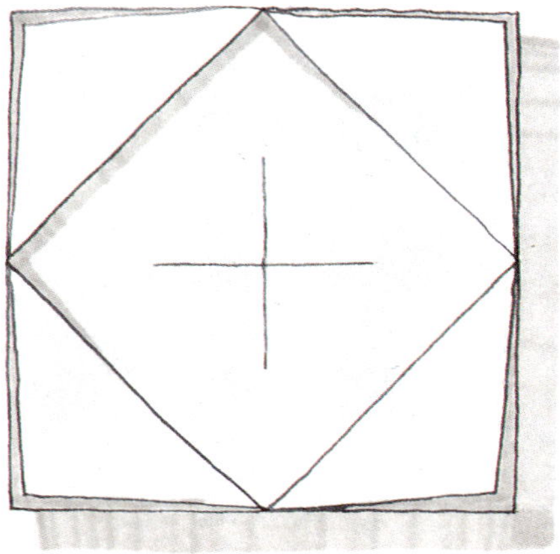

3 Trim your photograph to fit into the frame. Check that the area you want to see fits into the space available. If the paper you have used is quite stiff, the bottom flap at the back of the frame can be opened up to make the photo stand.

Candy Dish

Make individual sweet or nut cups for all the guests at the next birthday party. They will be intrigued to take them home as party favours and perhaps try to puzzle out how you made them. If you make them all in different papers, guests will be able to remember which one is theirs.

You will need:

A square of paper, preferably coloured on both sides, with sides between 15cm and 25cm (6in and 10in) long

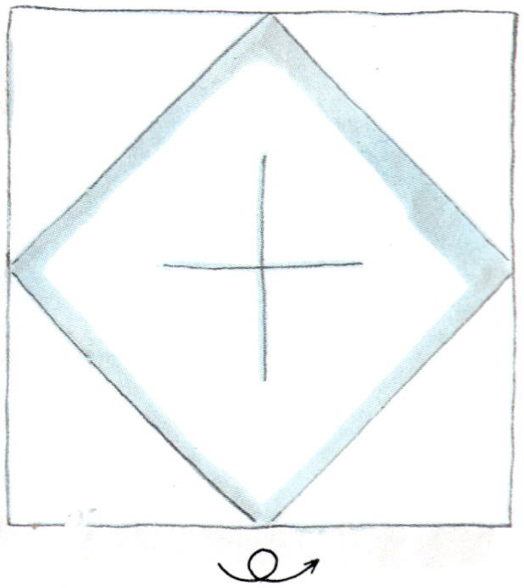

1 If the paper is coloured on one side only, begin with the white side up. Fold the frame. Turn it over from back to front.

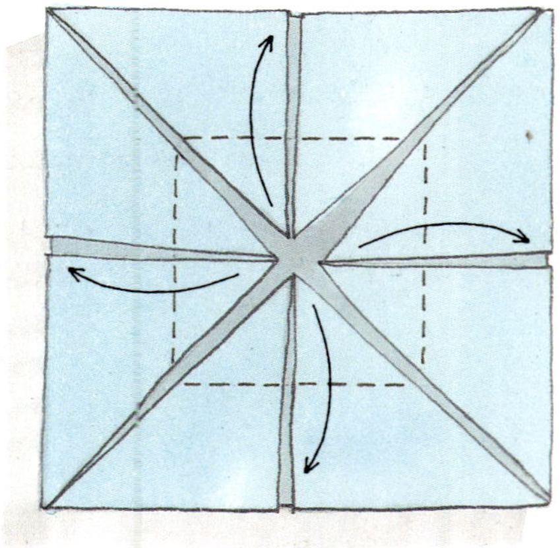

2 Fold the four corners from the centre to the outside edges.

3 Turn the paper over.

4 Push the forefinger of you left hand under one of the triangles. With your other thumb and forefinger squeeze the edges of the triangle to make it open up. Repeat this with the other three corners. This is not difficult, but tricky. Read over the instructions carefully and you'll find it will come out all right. Push and squeeze a little at the end to even the design. Look underneath and square the bottom.

Christmas Ornament

Use a square between 16cm and 20cm (6in and 8in), preferable in duo-coloured foil giftwrap (see page 8). Fold the candy dish. Glue a glass ball inside.

Helpful Hint

When I teach this sequence of four different things, I recapitulate the steps in brief. Students tell me this helps them remember all the steps for the candy dish:
TO the centre (Greetings card)
TO the centre (Coaster)
FROM the centre (Frame)
FROM the centre (Candy dish)
Turn the paper over from front to back each time between steps.

Handbag or Wallet

You can make this in any size you want, depending on whether you need a convenient wallet or an elegant evening bag to match an outfit.

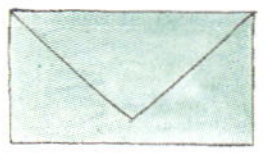

You will need:

For a wallet about 15cm (6in) wide:
a piece of giftwrap 30cm by 50cm (12in by 20in)
For a handbag about 23cm (9in) wide:
strong giftwrap or wall paper 45cm by 75cm (18in by 30in)
Self-fastening tape, such as Velcro (optional)

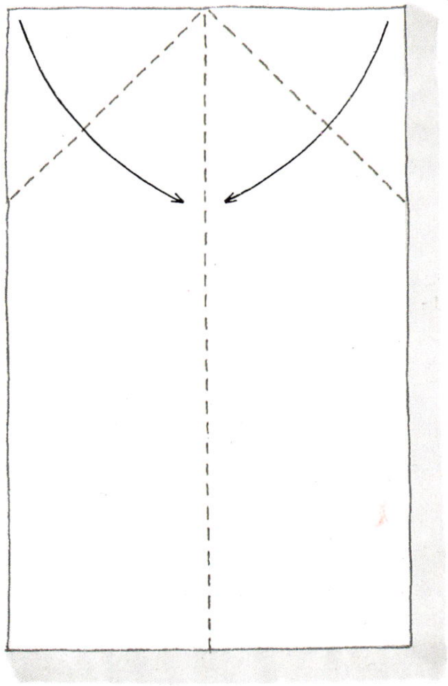

1 If the paper is coloured on one side only, begin with the white side up. Fold the paper in half lengthwise. Unfold. Fold two corners to the crease you have just made.

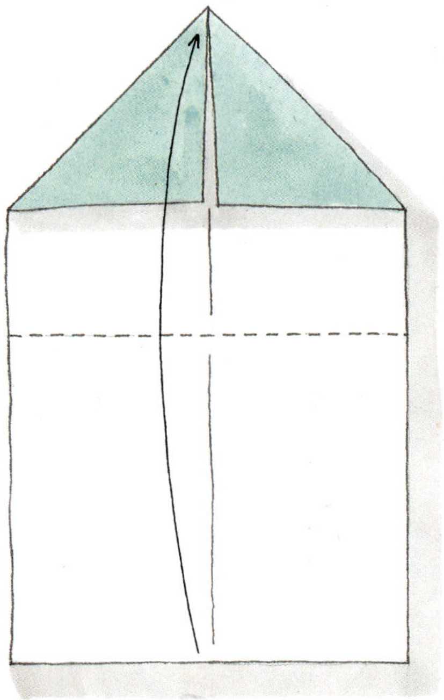

2 Fold the bottom edge up to the top point.

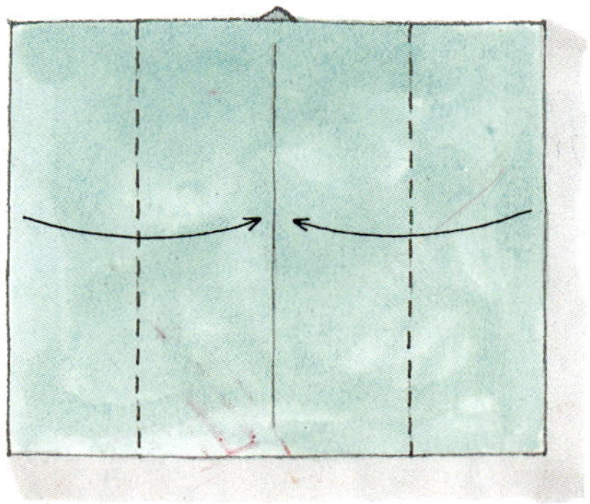

3 Fold the outer edges to the middle crease.

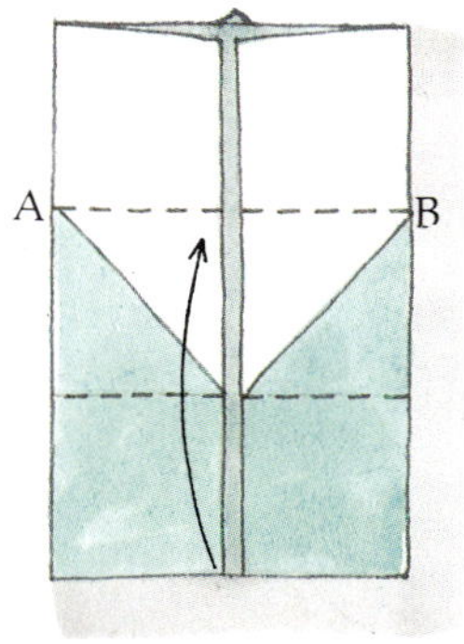

4 Fold the bottom edge to the line AB.

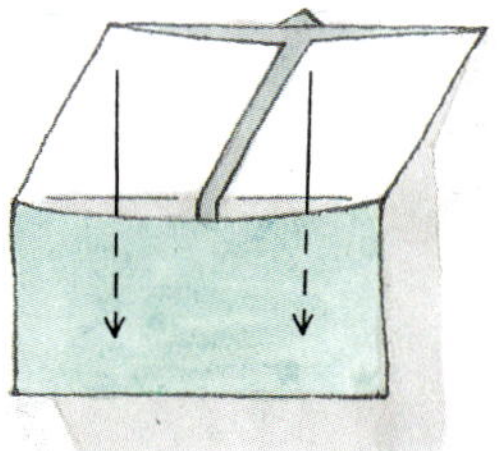

5 Carefully tuck the top flap into the front pocket.

6 You can, if you like, attach two small pieces of self-fastening tape to keep it closed.

Duck

The duck is an emblem of married happiness in oriental symbolism, because ducks pair for life and pine away when separated. What could be more appropriate than making ducks as decorations for a wedding or sending good wishes to an engaged couple with a card showing two ducks! You could add a short note explaining the sentiment. For the best effect, use Japanese handmade paper which imitates the texture of feathers.

You will need:

A square of giftwrap or other paper – you can use any size but 15cm (6in) works well

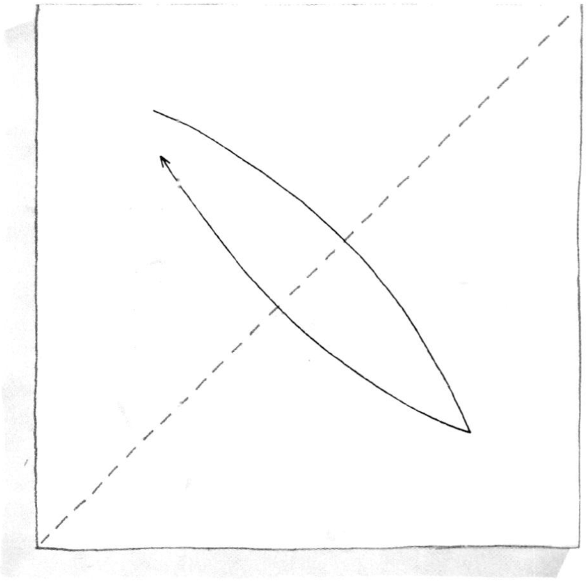

1 Fold the square along one of the diagonals. Unfold.

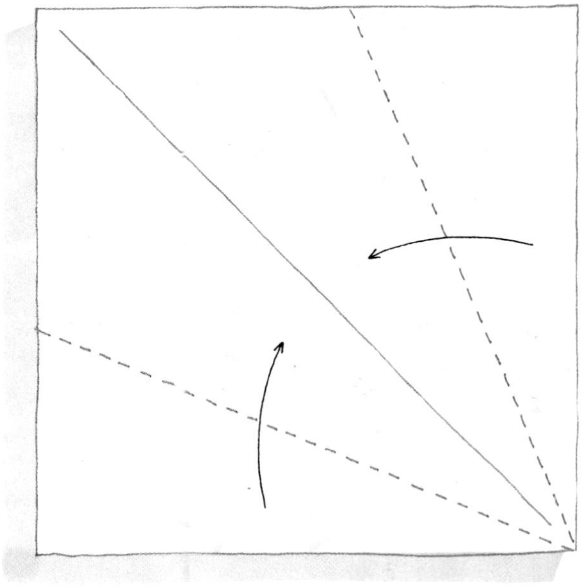

2 Fold two adjacent edges to the crease, as shown.

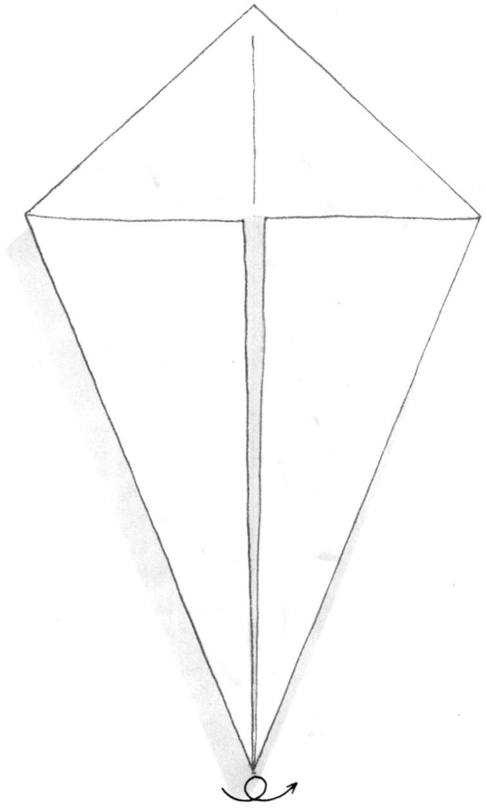

3 Turn the paper over.

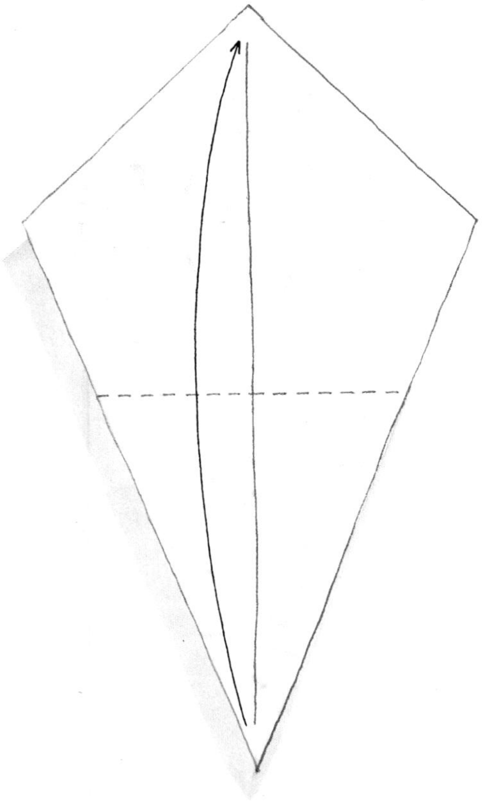

4 Fold the long point up to the wider point, as shown.

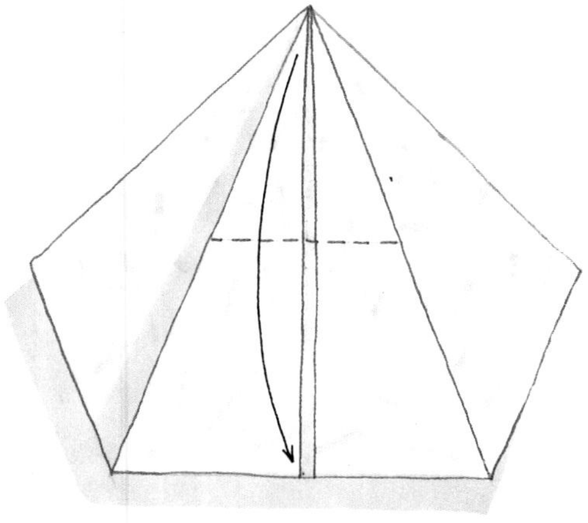

5 Fold the long point back to the edge.

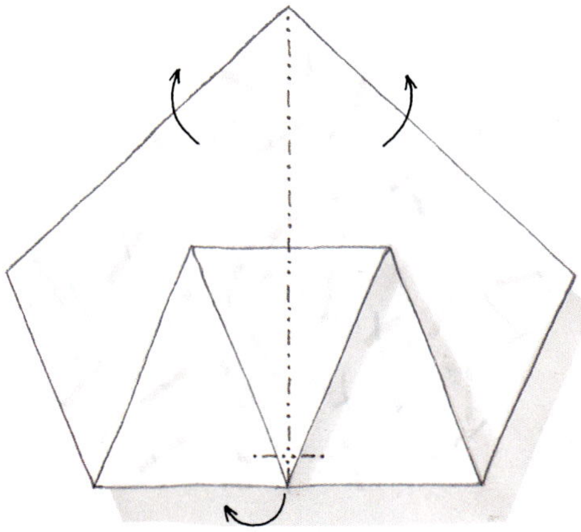

6 Blunt the tip by folding it under itself. Mountain fold the paper in half so that the head and neck are on the outside.

8 Crease a new fold at the front of the neck to keep it in place.

9 Pull the head forward until it is nearly horizontal. Crease a new fold at the back of the head to keep it in place.

7 Hold the body with one hand. Pull up the neck with the other hand until it is nearly upright.

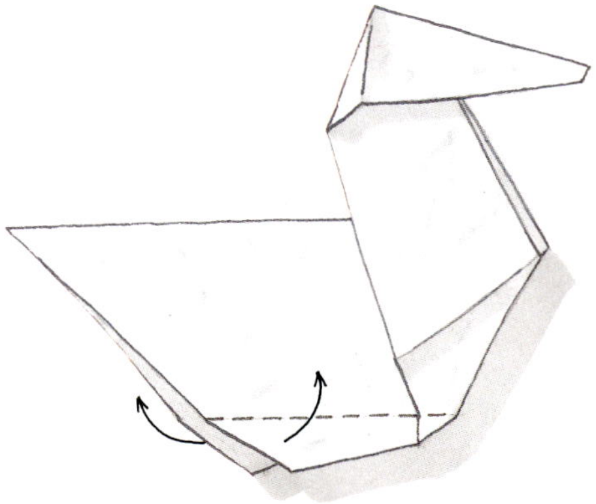

10 Fold up the feet. Place the feet flat on the ground so that the duck can stand. Draw on the beak and eyes with felt-tip pens.

Turkey

When creating origami animals, paperfolders try to portray any distinctive features. The turkey fulfils this aim by displaying a broad tail and a wattle at the throat. The turkey is fun to make at any time of the year but especially around Christmas or American Thanksgiving.

You will need:

A 15cm (6in) square of brown giftwrap or origami paper
A strip of giftwrap in a contrasting colour, 8cm by 70cm (3½in by 25in)
Sticky tape

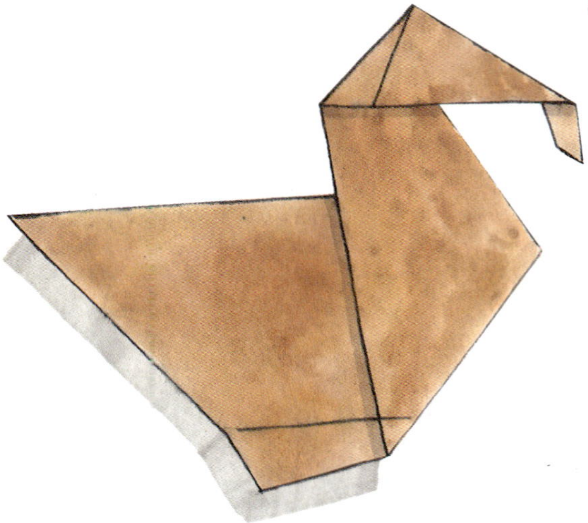

1 Fold a duck from the square, following the instructions on page 66. Make a wattle by folding the tip of the beak over and down, as shown.

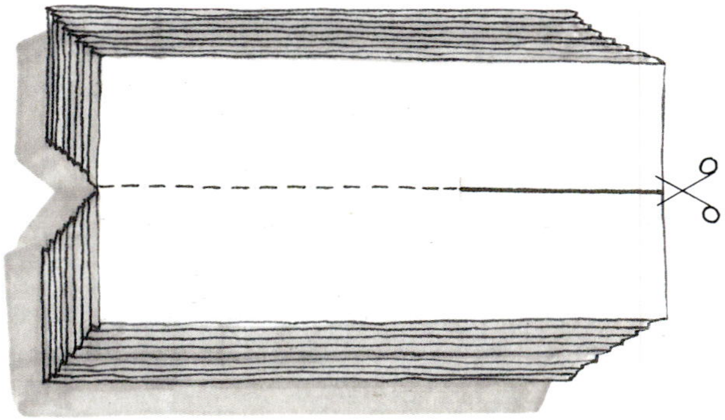

2 Fan pleat the strip of paper into 2cm (¾in) pleats. Cut a 2½cm (1in) slit in the middle of the pleated fan.

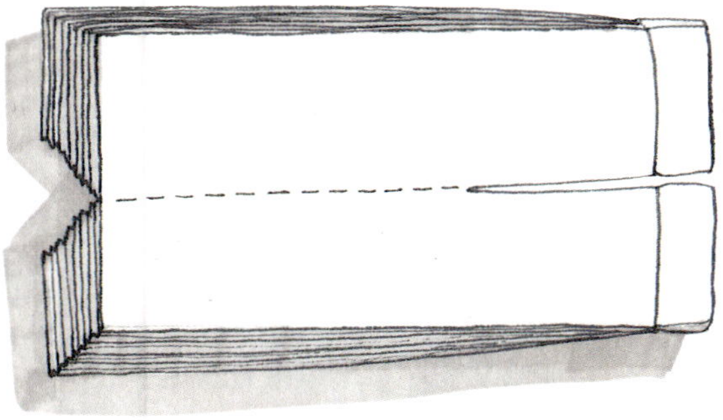

3 Wind a very narrow piece of tape around each bunch of pleats on either side of the slit.

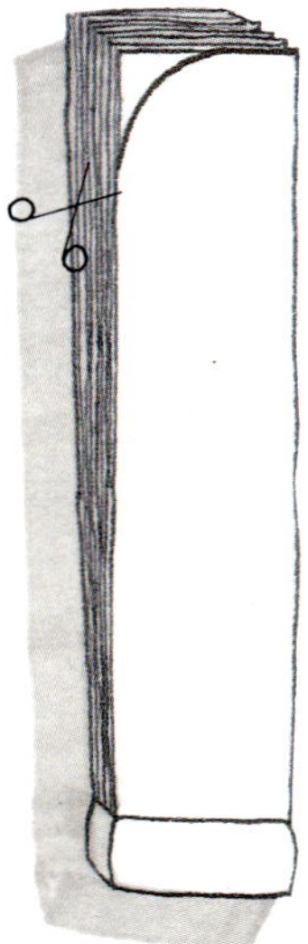

4 Cut a curve at the top of the pleated fan through all the layers. If the paper is too heavy to cut all the layers at once, then cut half the pleats at a time.

5 Spread the fan and place it over the bird. If you like, you can tape or staple the fan tail to the body.

All-Purpose Card

Need a card this minute? Here is a quick way to turn a piece of paper into a greetings card. You can use stationery, giftwrap or almost any other kind of paper. Depending on how much time you have, just write your greeting with a felt-tip pen, or decorate the front and inside with paper patchwork (see page 20) or origami.

You will need:
A piece of paper
Felt-tip pen

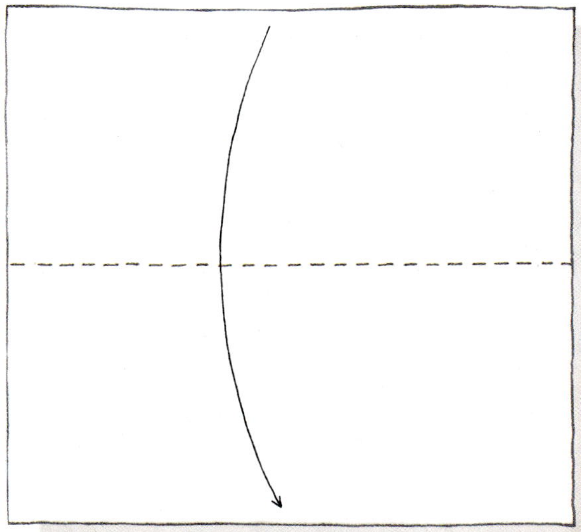

1 Write your greeting boldly on the paper. Fold the paper in half lengthwise.

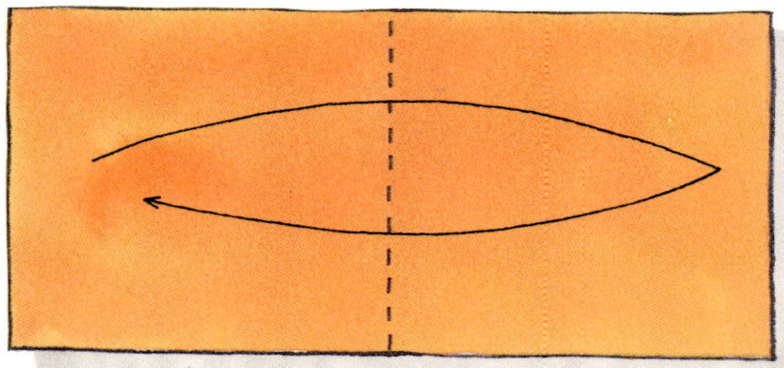

2 Fold in half. Unfold.

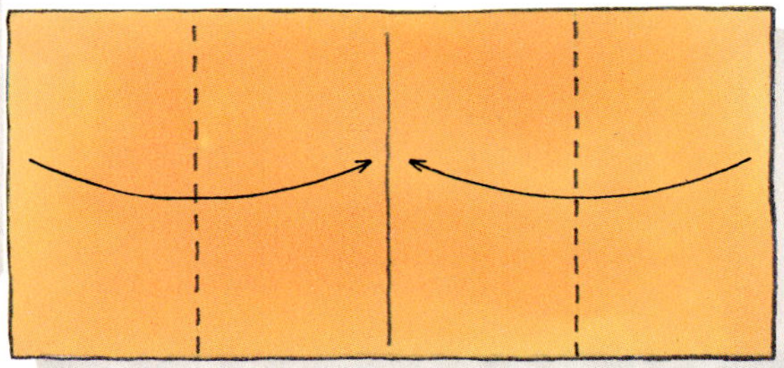

3 Fold the short outside edges to the crease just made.

4 Fold the paper in half. Decorate the front and inside panels.

Place Cards

Fold the all-purpose card from a piece of paper 20cm by 15cm (8in by 6in). Slide one end of the card into the other. Write the name on the front.

Flower

Origami flowers have a charm of their own because they do not pretend to be real but remind us of the beauty of nature. Display them in a vase or make an asymmetrical arrangement as a semi-permanent or temporary decoration. You will probably find many ways to use the flowers and derive enormous satisfaction in crafting them.

You will need:

Origami squares or duo-coloured paper between 10cm and 15cm square (4in and 6in)
Toothpick or knitting needle
Green paper or pipe-cleaner or floral wire ***(see page 10)******, green floral tape***

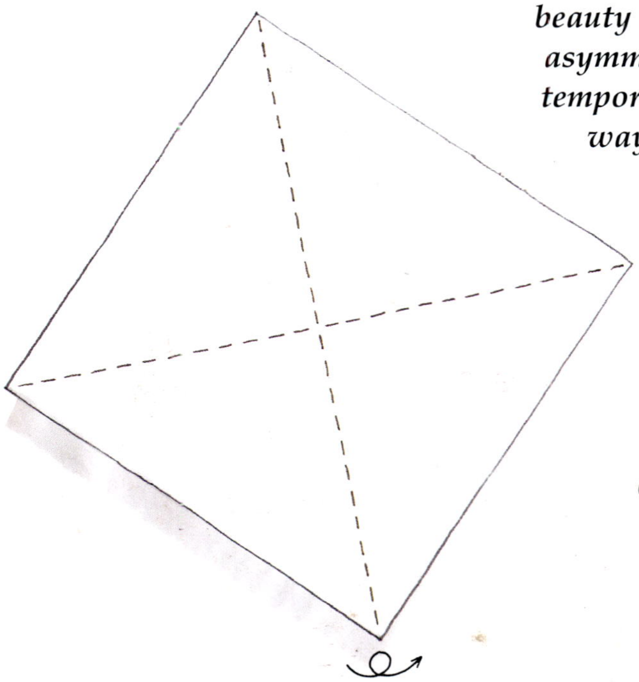

1 Fold the square on both diagonals. Unfold the paper flat each time. Turn the paper over.

2 Fold the paper in half and unfold. Fold the paper in half the other way and leave folded.

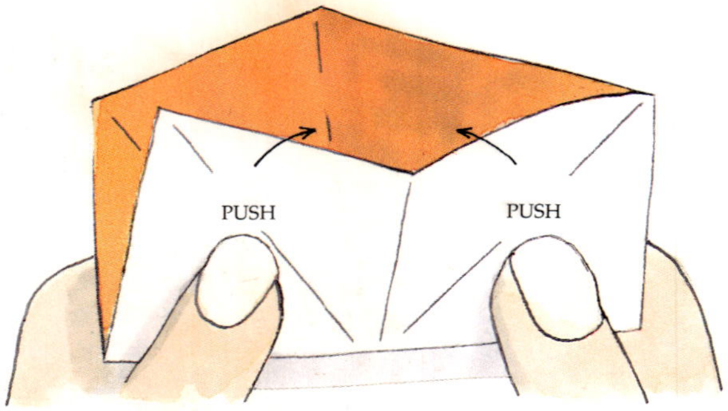

3 Hold the folded edge with both hands exactly where shown. Move your hands towards each other until the paper forms a square. Fold the front flap to one side and the back flap to the other side.

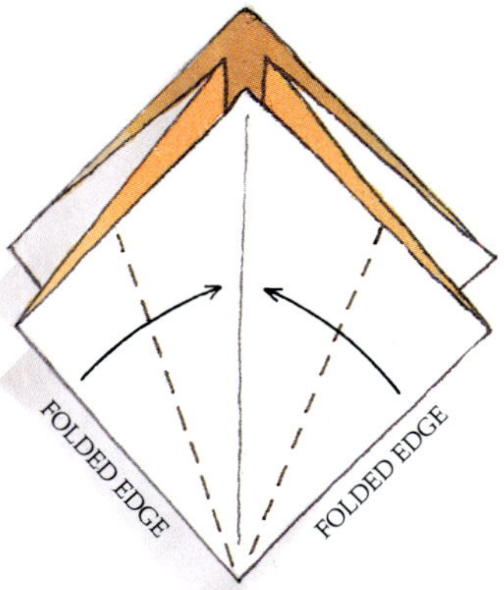

4 For the next step, on the front flaps only, make guide creases by bringing the folded outside edges to the middle. Then unfold them.

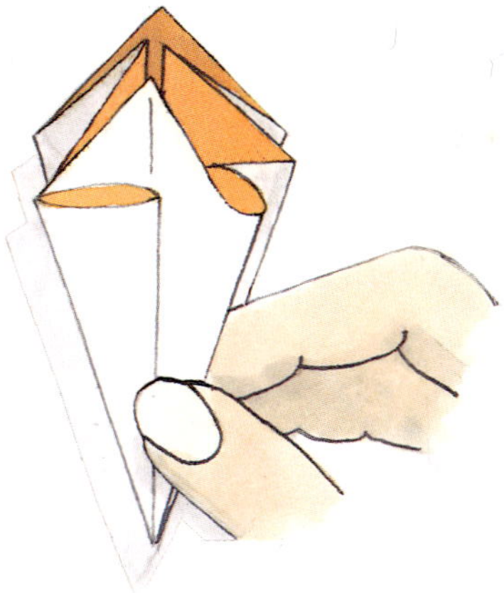

5 On the same creases, tuck the left outside edge behind the front layer of paper. The paper opens up a little as you do this. Crease sharply on the guide creases. Repeat with the right side. Turn the paper over and repeat on the back.

Boutonniere

Wear a buttonhole made from 5cm (2in) paper squares. Use different colours, but test the papers first for colour fastness. Make each square into a flower and then wind green sewing thread around the stems to hold the flowers together.

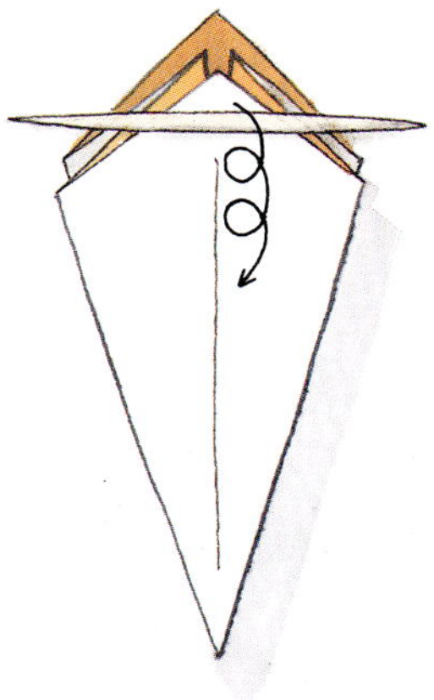

6 Roll the triangle at the top over the toothpick. Repeat on the back.

7 Open up the flower and roll the other two petals over the toothpick.

8 Make the stem from the pipe-cleaner or floral wire covered in green floral tape. Roll one end of the stem over the toothpick.

9 Or you can make a stem by rolling a strip of green paper tightly on the diagonal, beginning over a toothpick. Curl the wider end of the finished stem to stop it unrolling.

10 Cut a snip off the bottom of the flower and insert the stem so the curled end is inside the flower.

Flowers in a Vase

Make several flowers, perhaps of different colours. Cut the wired stems to the required lengths using wire cutters or pliers. In the arrangement shown here, the cup is filled with floral styrofoam. The narrow leaves are cut from green paper and the ends taped to the floral wire.

Flower Napkin Ring

Add an elegant touch to the dinner table with napkin rings decorated with origami flowers. For a well co-ordinated look make them from paper in colours which appear in the napkins.

You will need:

A strip of giftwrap paper 20cm by 8cm (8in by 3in)
Two origami flowers made from squares of paper not larger than 7cm (3in)
Glue

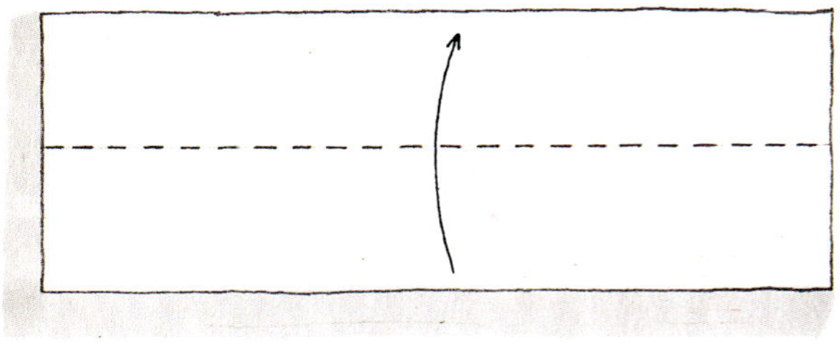

1 Fold the strip of giftwrap in half lengthwise. Unfold.

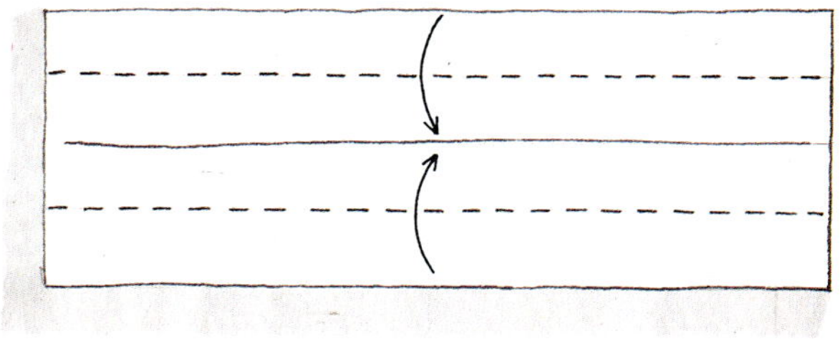

2 Fold the two long edges to the middle.

3 Glue on the two origami flowers.

4 Bend the strip into a napkin ring and slide one end into the other.

Fancy Flower Hat

Fast to make and fun to wear! These hats will work for many occasions from costumes at school plays to family parties. Everyone will enjoy folding them and jazzing them up with lots of add-ons. Depending on the occasion use ordinary or foil giftwrap and strengthen thin paper by using it double.

You will need:

Giftwrap or newspaper – 40cm (16in) square
Sticky tape, glue
Decorations (see below)
Elastic or coloured ribbon

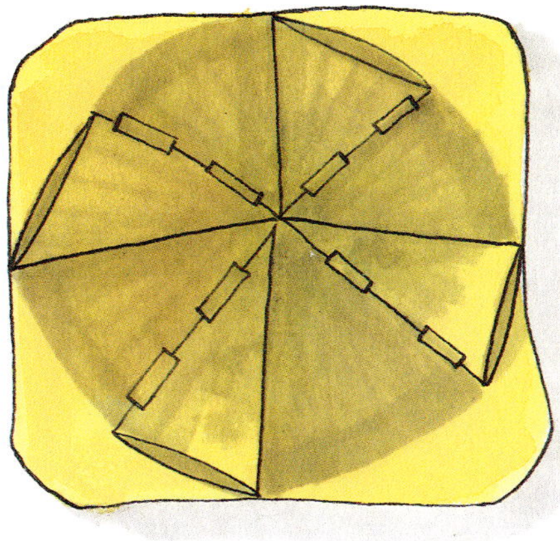

1 Follow the directions for folding the flower (see page 70). Tape the inside seams flat. Glue the outside seams.

2 Glue on small origami flowers, animals, confetti, stickers, sequins, paper strips and any other decorations.

3 Attach elastic or coloured ribbon to each side to keep the hat on.

Tray and Basket

In some small European towns bakers still package biscuits, chocolates and cakes in this traditional tray. When they are not busy they fold some ahead, stack them flat and open them up quickly when needed. You can make them in any size for gifts or for organizing small items. Giftwrap makes the most beautiful trays. Use it double for added strength and so the pattern appears all over.

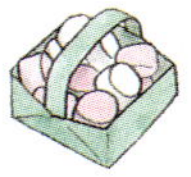

You will need:

A piece of giftwrap or other paper. You can use any size but the length should be twice the width – 30cm by 15cm (12in by 6in) is a good size to start with
Scissors

1 Fold the paper into quarters. Unfold. Cut off one quarter and keep it for a handle. You are left with three panels.

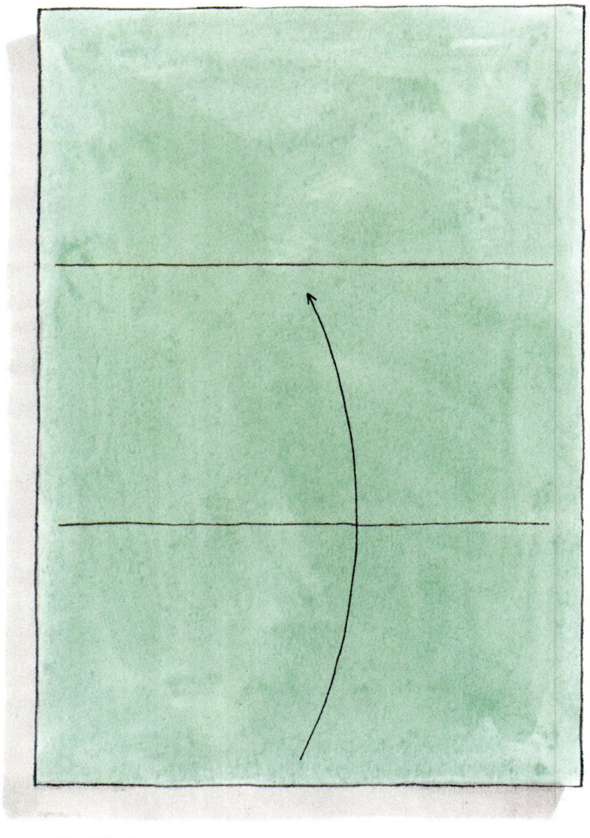

2 If the paper is coloured on one side only, place the coloured side up. Fold one panel over.

3 Fold this flap in half to find the middle. Open it out. Fold the four corners in, as shown.

Thrifty Method

If your tray does not need a handle, you can avoid cutting off the extra piece at the beginning. Fold the paper in thirds, either by measuring or by folding over both ends and manipulating it until all three layers are equal.

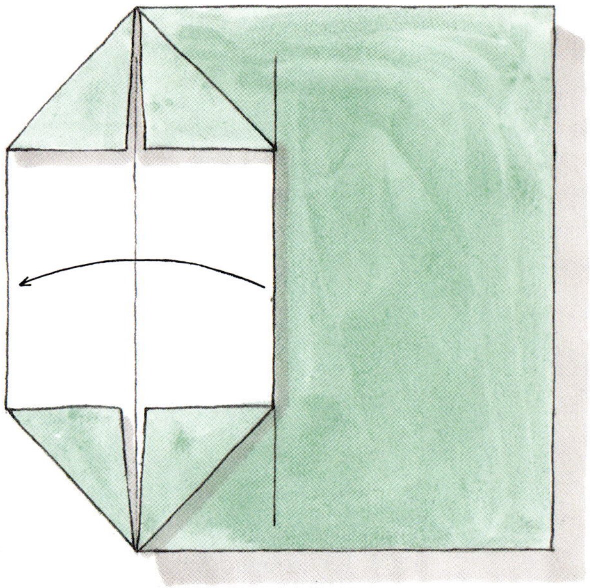

4 Fold the right half of the flap over the left.

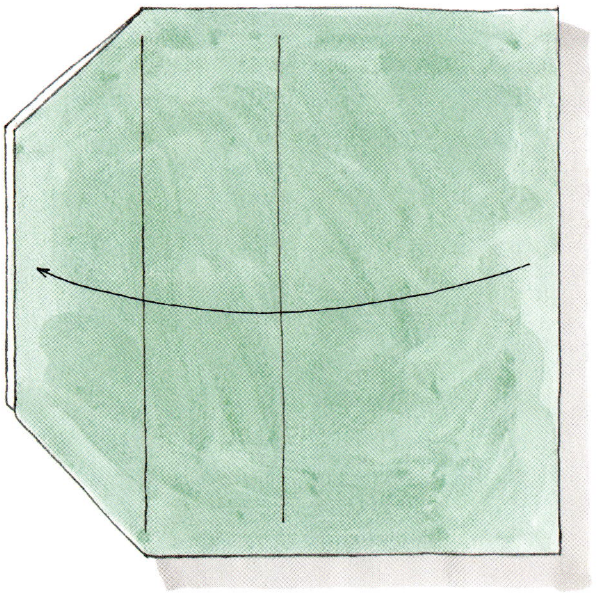

5 Fold the other side panel over.

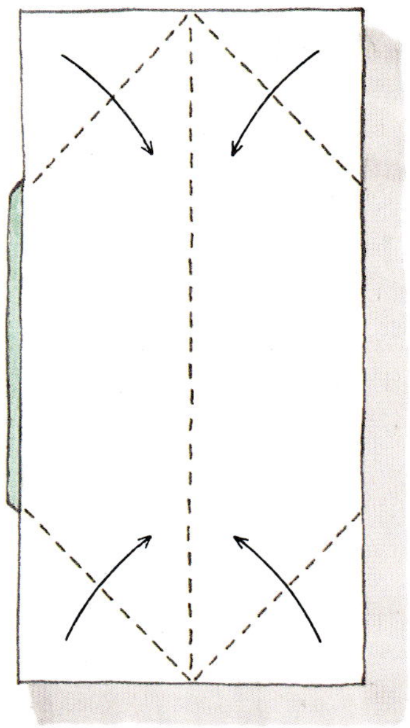

6 Fold the flap in half to find the middle. Fold in the four corners as before. Fold the flap in half from left to right.

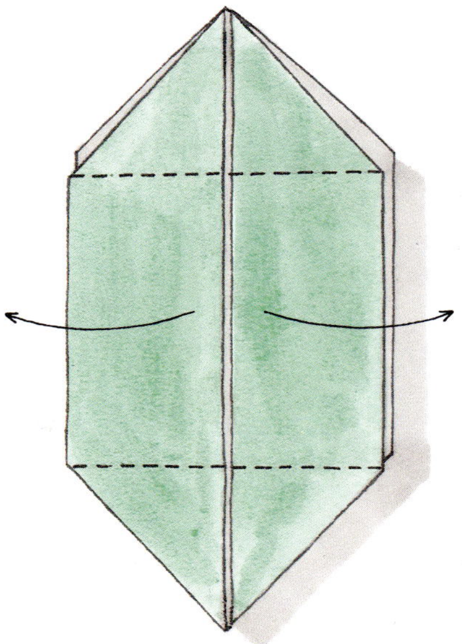

7 Crease the top and bottom triangles back and forth, as shown by the broken lines, but finish with the paper in the same position as before. Gently pull the edges from the middle to the outside.

8 Shape the box by creasing all the corners sharply.

Basket with a Handle

To make the tray into a basket, add a handle. Use the strip you cut off in step 1. Fold it over two or three times. Staple or tape it to the basket.

Gift Box

How many times have you tried to find a box just the right size for a gift? It is easy to make covered boxes. Use giftwrap paper or other coloured papers. Here you will even find out the secret of determining the right size you need.

You will need:
Two pieces of paper
Scissors

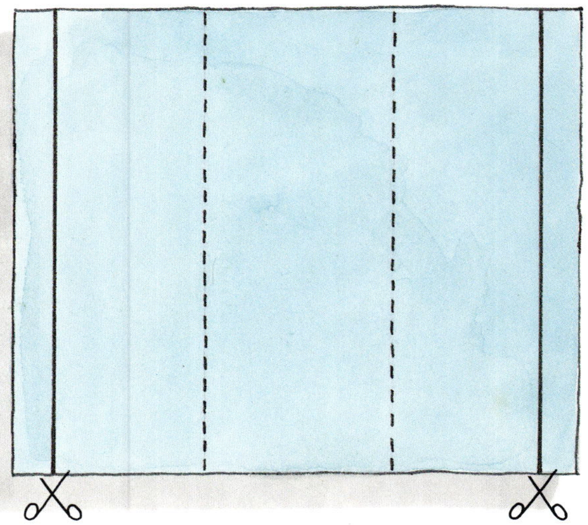

The Right Size

You can predict the final size of your box. As directed, begin with a piece of paper twice as long as it is wide. Divide the smaller number in half. This will be the square size of the finished box.

1 The bottom of the box has to be a little smaller than the lid. Cut two pieces of paper the same size. From one piece cut off ¾cm (¼in) from one long side and from one short side.

2 Fold both papers into trays. Fit them into each other.

Different Sizes

The sides of the box can be lowered. Before step 3 of the tray, cut some paper off both side edges. Then proceed as usual. Do the same thing when you make the lid.

Display Case

Use a box on its side to display origami models or other small treasures. The lid will keep everything safe for storing or taking from place to place.

Cactus in Bloom

A cactus brings to mind wide open spaces and the Big Sky. You can suggest this atmosphere with origami cacti. Set three blooming ones on sand-coloured paper for an interesting table decoration. You might even use rough household sandpaper. A giant cactus set in the corner of a room may become a real conversation piece, especially when people realize it is made from paper.

You will need:

A piece of green paper 25cm (10in) square
Yellow writing paper (same colour on both sides) cut into one 6cm (2½in) square and three 5cm (2in) squares
Glue

Giant Cactus

For a larger decoration, fold a cactus from Canson Mi-teinte paper. Sharpen the creases in this heavy paper by going over them with the end of a ruler. Try these size squares – 50cm (20in) green, 12cm and 10cm (5in and 4in) yellow.

1 Fan pleat the green paper into eight ribs, by first folding the paper in half, in half again and then in half again (see page 12).

2 Fold the corner of the first pleat in as shown.

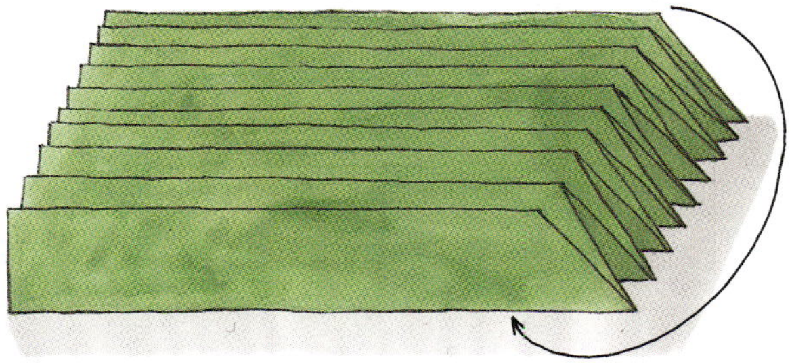

3 Unfold the corner and push it to the inside of the pleat. Repeat with all the other pleats.

4 Roll the fan into a column and overlap the two end pleats. The indented tops hook neatly over each other. If you like, you can glue the ends together lightly.

5 Fold four flowers from the yellow squares as shown on page 70. Place the larger flower with a smaller flower inside it in the hole at the top of the cactus. Glue the other two flowers to the edges of the cactus.

Earrings

You can never have too many earrings. Once you know how to make origami earrings you can have a pair to match the colours of every outfit. Use foil giftwrap or handmade paper, both of which can take a lot of wear, or any paper in the right colour. If you like, you can varnish the earrings. And don't forget to give them as presents, perhaps in an origami box.

You will need:

Two 5cm (2in) squares of duo-coloured paper
Earring fittings (see page 11) or thread

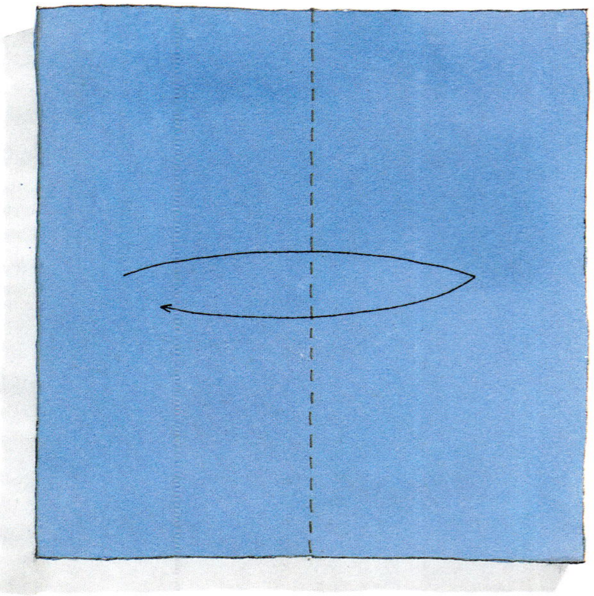

1 Fold one of the squares from side to side. Unfold.

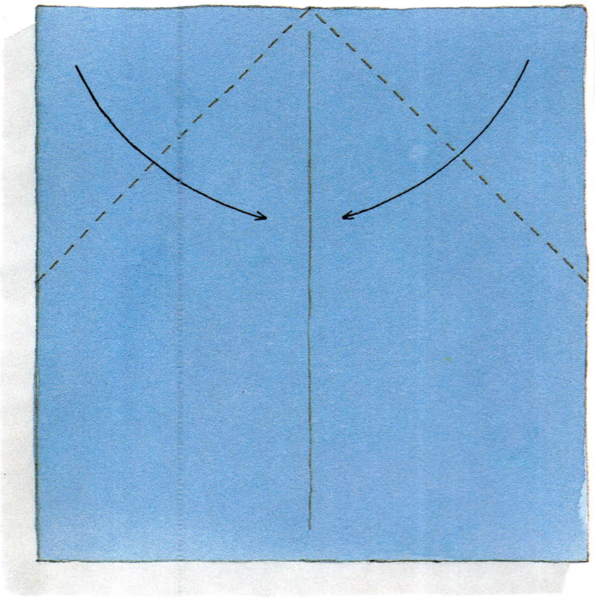

2 Fold two corners to the middle crease.

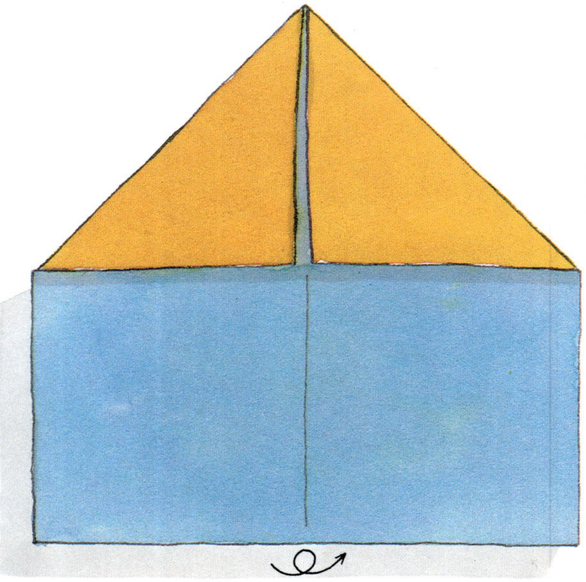

3 Turn the paper over.

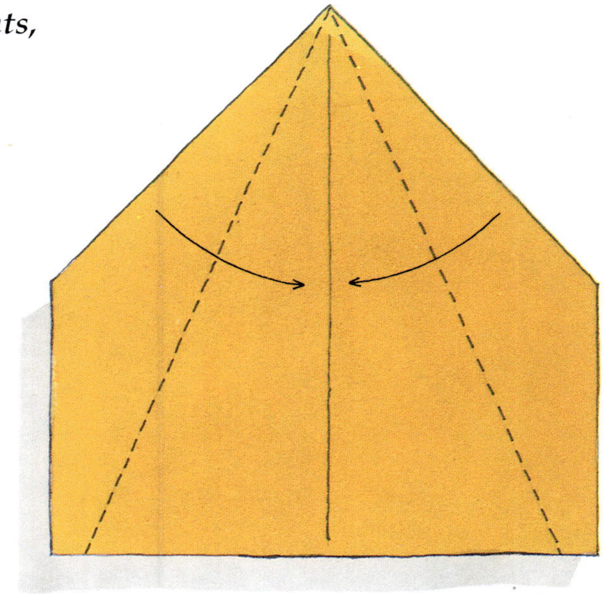

4 Fold the slanted edges to the middle.

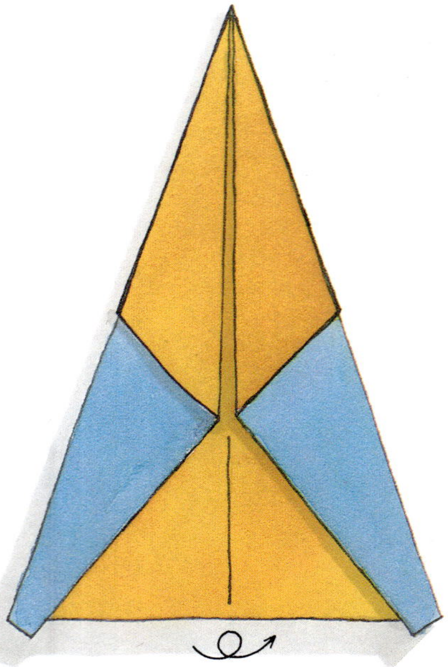

5 Turn the paper over.

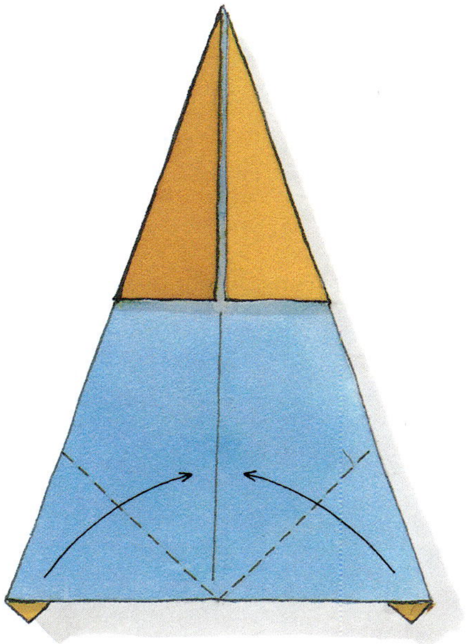

6 Fold the lower corners to the middle. The two small triangles overlap.

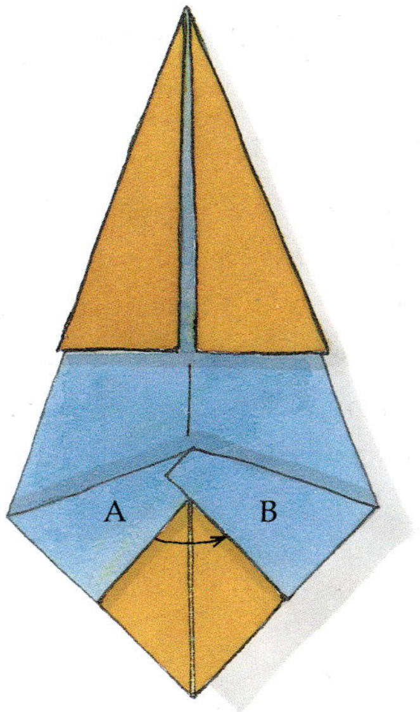

7 Make the earring three-dimensional by overlapping A and B. You can tuck A into B, or glue them together. Fold back the outside edge of the top flaps to touch the long edge of the earring. This pushes the front of the earring out.

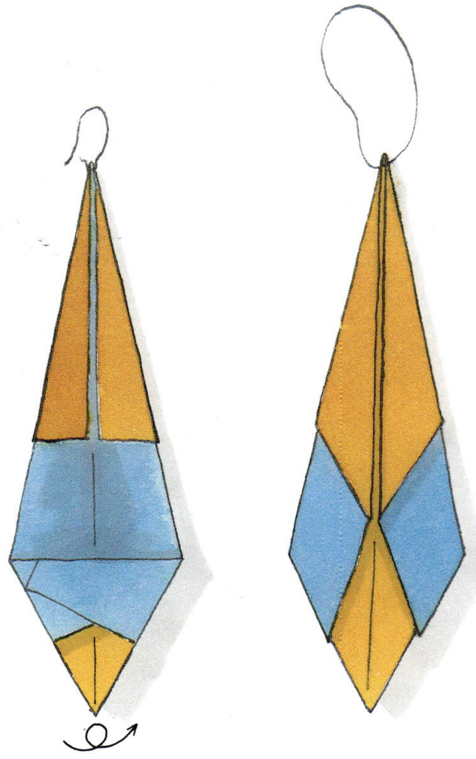

8 Make the other earring from the other square of paper. Attach earring fittings or a loop of thread to hang over the ears.

Hanging Ornament

You will need a 10cm (4in) duo-coloured foil giftwrap square (see page 8). Follow the instructions for folding the earring. Attach a loop of thread or wire hook to hang up the ornament. It can be hung singly or several of them can be joined to make a mobile.

Bowl of Fruit

A classic origami whose origin is well buried in the past is the waterbomb or ball. It has a surprise feature: after all the folds are completed it can be blown up into a three-dimensional ball. This classic pattern is adapted here to making oranges, apples and grapes which are arranged in a bowl made according to the directions for the candy dish on page 64. Origami paper can be used for all the fruit, but coloured printing paper from photocopy shops may be substituted for the oranges and apples. Foil giftwrap gives the grapes an appropriate glossy appearance.

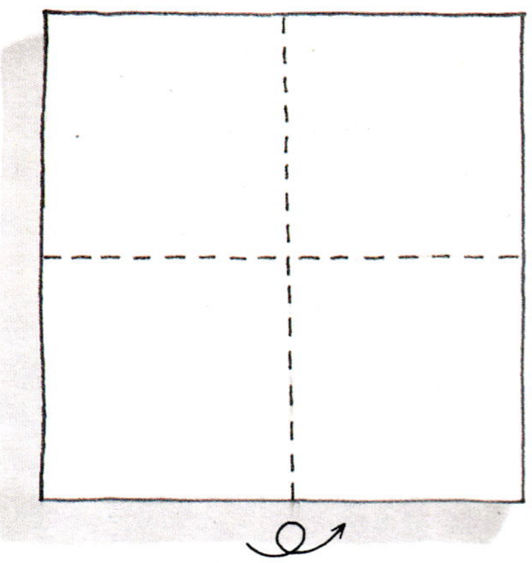

The Orange

1 To make the orange, use the orange paper. If it is coloured on one side only, begin with the coloured side up. Fold the square in half in both directions. Unfold flat each time. Turn the paper from front to back.

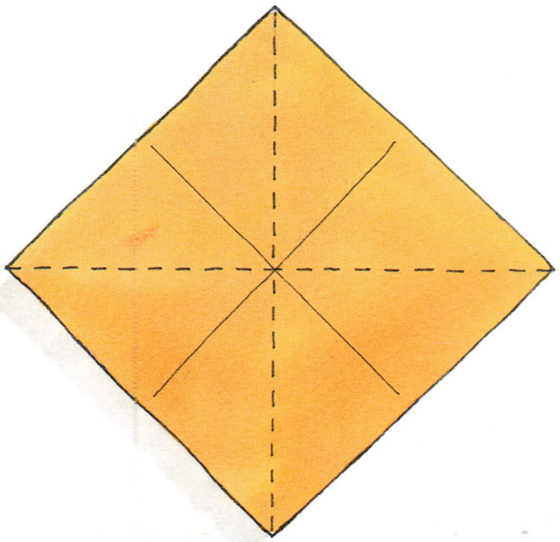

2 Fold from corner to corner on the diagonal. Unfold. Fold on the other diagonal. Leave folded.

You will need:

For an orange, *a 20cm (8in) orange origami paper square*
For an apple, *a 20cm (8in) red origami paper square*
For the apple stem, *a small piece of duo-coloured brown paper*
For the apple leaf, *a small piece of duo-coloured green paper*
Pencil, scissors, glue
For a bunch of grapes, *nine 6cm or 8cm (2in or 3in) light green or purple origami paper squares*
Needle and thread
For the bowl, *a 50cm (20in) square of duo-coloured giftwrap*
A piece of green tissue paper

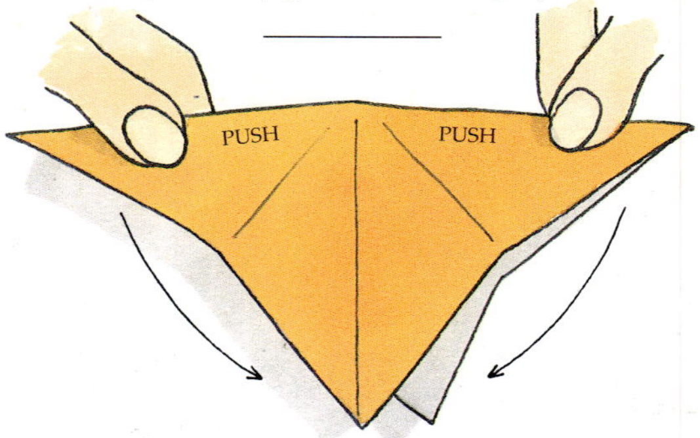

3 Hold the paper exactly as shown. Push your hands down. Fold the front flap to the right. Fold the back flap to the left. You now have a triangle.

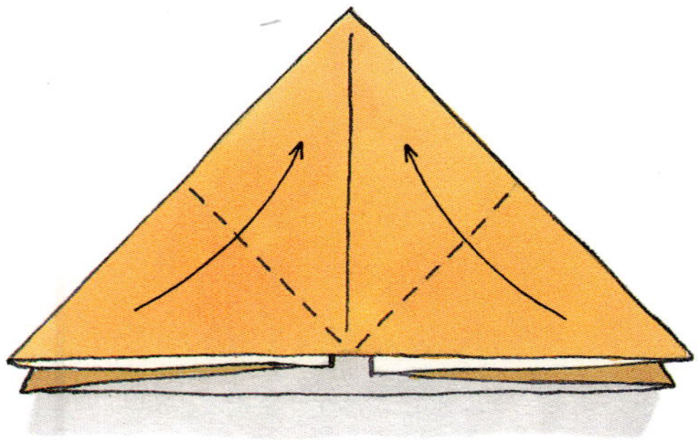

4 This is called the waterbomb base. Fold the two outer corners up on the front flaps only. Turn the paper over and repeat on the back.

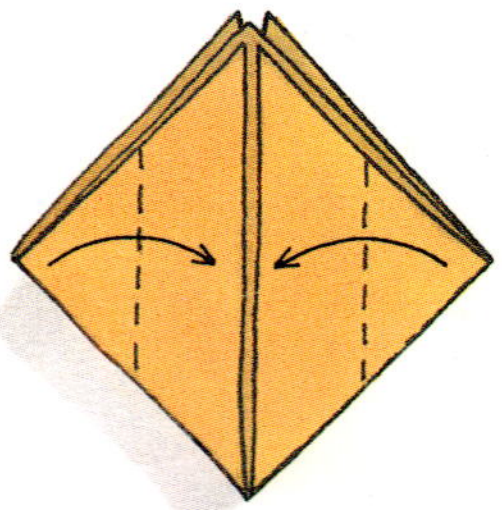

5 On the front flaps only, bring the outer corners to the middle. Turn the paper over and repeat on the back.

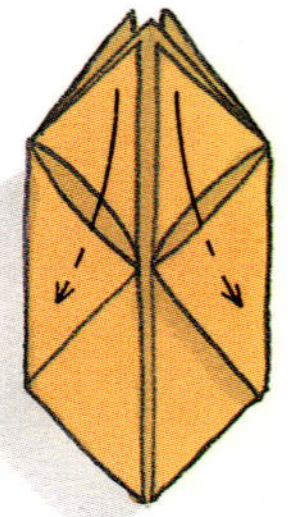

6 Arrange the paper so that the loose points are at the top. Tuck the two loose points on the front into the pockets of the triangles as far as you can. They do not go in all the way. Turn the paper over and repeat on the back.

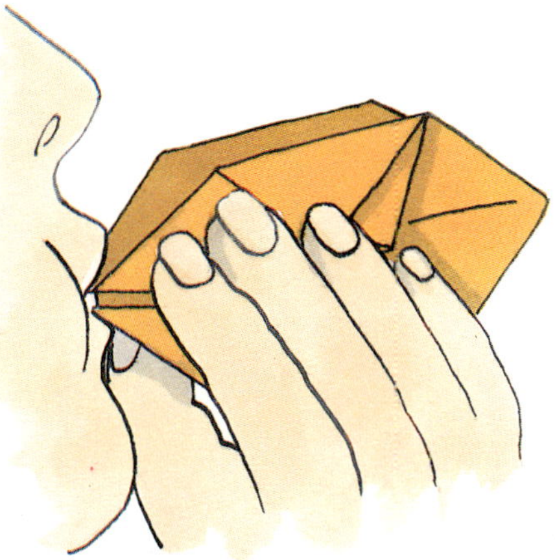

7 Inflate the paper by holding the ball between your fingers and thumbs. Put the open end to your mouth. Blow in the opening. Now you have made the orange.

The Apple

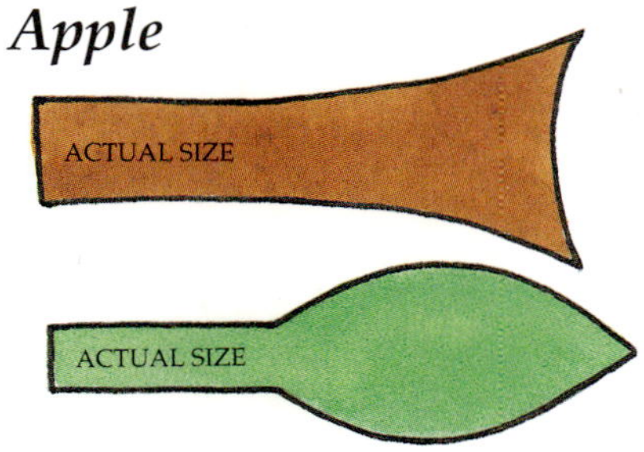

8 To make the apple, use red paper and follow all the steps for the orange. Trace the stem and leaf patterns on the brown and green papers. Cut them out.

9 Glue the leaf to the stem.

10 Slide the stem in between the two layers of paper at the top of the apple and squeeze in a drop of glue. Bend the stem and leaf upright.

The Bunch of Grapes

11 To make the bunch of grapes, use the light green or purple paper and fold nine grapes following all the steps for the orange. String them into a bunch with a needle and thread. Catch the corner of each grape by pushing the threaded needle in and out. When all the grapes are gathered, knot together both ends of the thread. The grapes will form into a bunch.

The Bowl

12 To make the bowl follow the instructions for the candy dish.

13 To assemble the display, make three oranges, four apples and two bunches of grapes. Line the bottom of the bowl with crushed green tissue paper. Arrange the fruit on top.

Peace Crane

The crane is probably the best known model in origami and has become a symbol of peace. It is of intermediate difficulty, but if you follow the directions carefully you should have no problem in completing it. It will be well worth your effort. Step 3 forms what is known as the bird base. It is the jumping off point for many other designs.

You will need:

An origami square between 15cm and 20cm (6in and 8in)

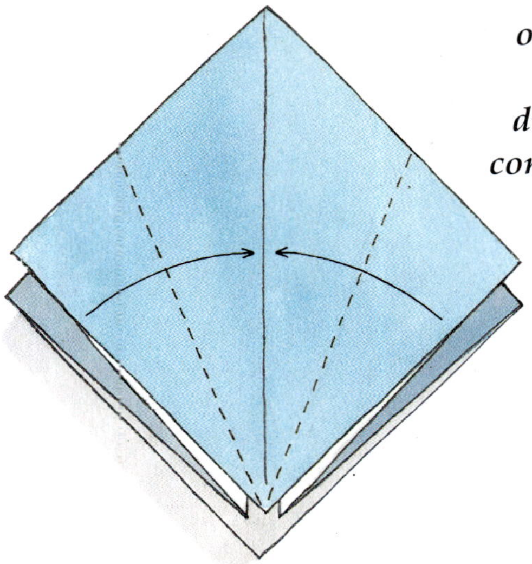

1 Fold the first three steps of the flower as shown on page 70. Place the paper with the closed corner at the top. Fold the raw edges (not folded edges) of the front flaps to the centre crease. Turn the paper over and repeat with the two flaps on the back.

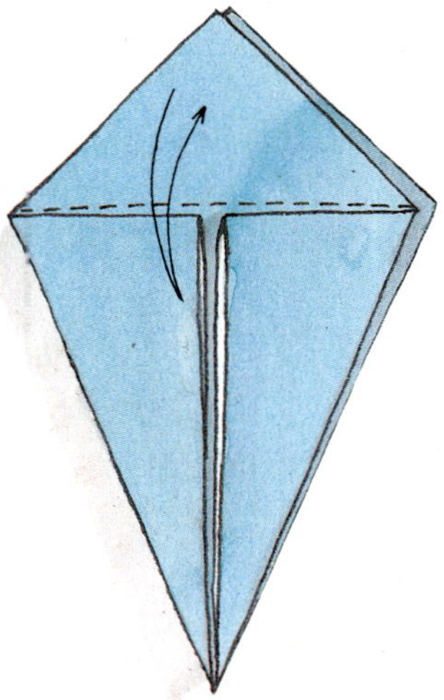

2 Fold the triangle at the top forward and backward, bringing it back to its original position. This makes a helpful crease for the next step.

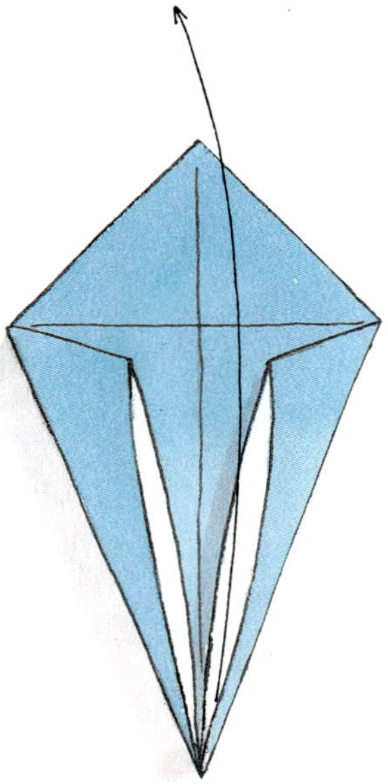

3 Open the front flaps slightly. This exposes the corner of the paper at the bottom tip. Lift it up in the direction of the arrow until you are able to fold the paper on the helpful crease you made in step 2. The outer edges of the paper will move to the middle as you proceed and form a diamond. Flatten the paper – see next drawing. Turn the paper over and repeat on the back. (Paperfolders call this the bird base.)

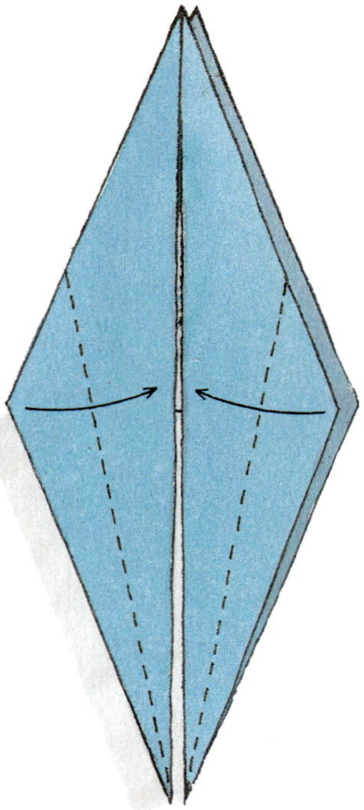

4 Fold the outer edges to the middle, first on the front flaps. Then turn the paper over and repeat on the back.

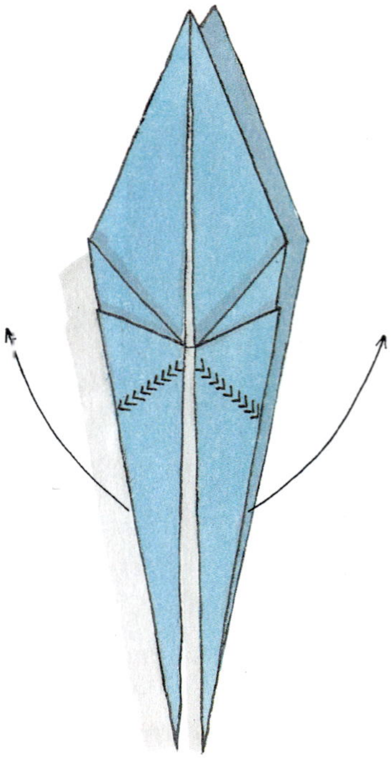

5 Bring the two flaps up in between the two main layers of paper. (Paperfolders call this a reverse fold.)

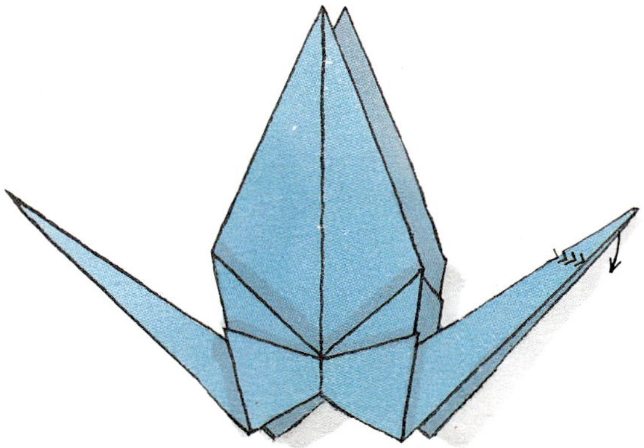

6 Reverse fold the head in between the two layers of the neck.

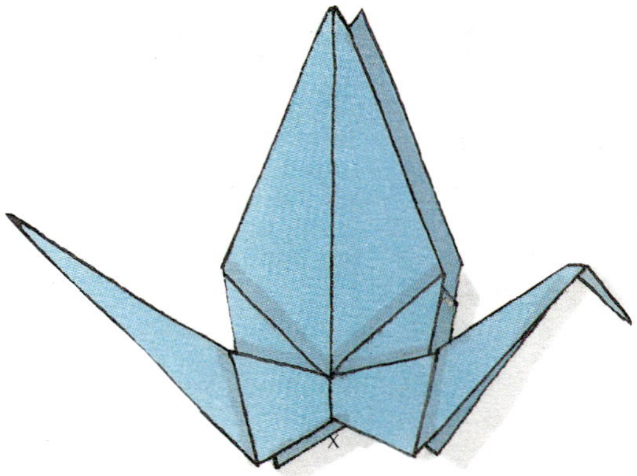

7 Inflate the crane by holding a wing in each hand. Pull gently apart and at the same time blow into the opening at X.

Millions of children have heard about 12-year old Sadako Sasaki who tried to fold 1000 cranes. She lived in Hiroshima, Japan, at the time when the atomic bomb was dropped and suffered radiation sickness. According to a Japanese custom folding 1000 cranes will bring good health and good luck. Unfortunately Sadaki was unable to complete the task. Others not only finished it for her but a memorial bearing her likeness holding a crane was erected in Hiroshima. Children from all over the world send chains of folded cranes to the memorial to promote peace everywhere.

Crane Toy

Knot the bird to a length of string. Attach the other end of the string to a dowel stick. When you wave the stick around the bird seems to fly. As an added attraction add some ribbon.

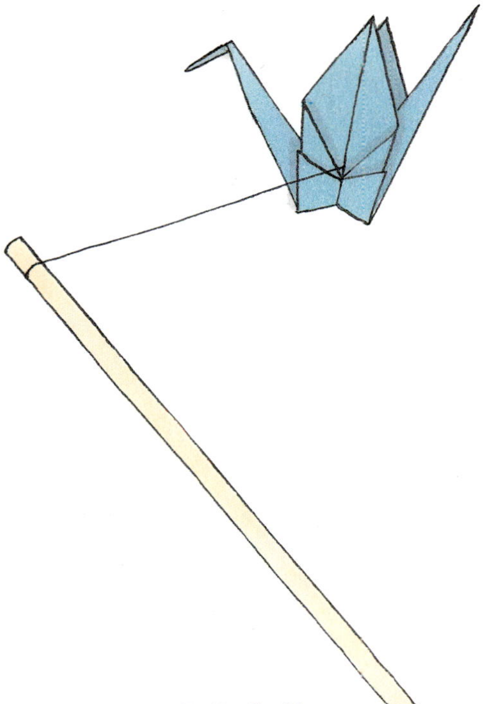

Mobile

Make the crane from pastel coloured paper and hang it over a baby's crib. Thread it through the top of the body before blowing it up.

The Flapping Bird

The flapping bird is an amusing action toy that is a variation of the classic crane. You will always amaze anyone for whom you fold it.

You will need:

An origami paper square between 15cm and 20cm (6in and 8in)

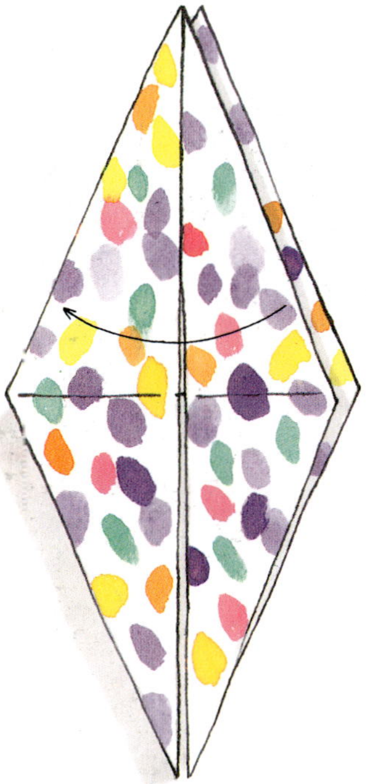

1 Fold the first three steps of the crane on page 82, making a bird base. Fold the top flap only from right to left like turning the pages of a book. Turn the paper over and repeat on the back, again folding from right to left.

2 Fold the bottom flap up as far as it will go. Turn the paper over and repeat on the back.

3 Pull the hidden points in the direction of the arrows, one at a time. To make them stay in the position shown in the next drawing, crease sharply as shown by the dotted lines.

4 Reverse fold the head down in between the two layers of the neck. To flap the wings, hold it at X with one hand and gently pull the tail back and forth. Do not pull it up and down.

Helpful Hint

The wings will not always work on the first try. In that case try flapping by holding at the Y instead of the X. If this still does not work, reach down between the body of the bird and the wing, as far as you can; wiggle the wing. Do this with both wings.

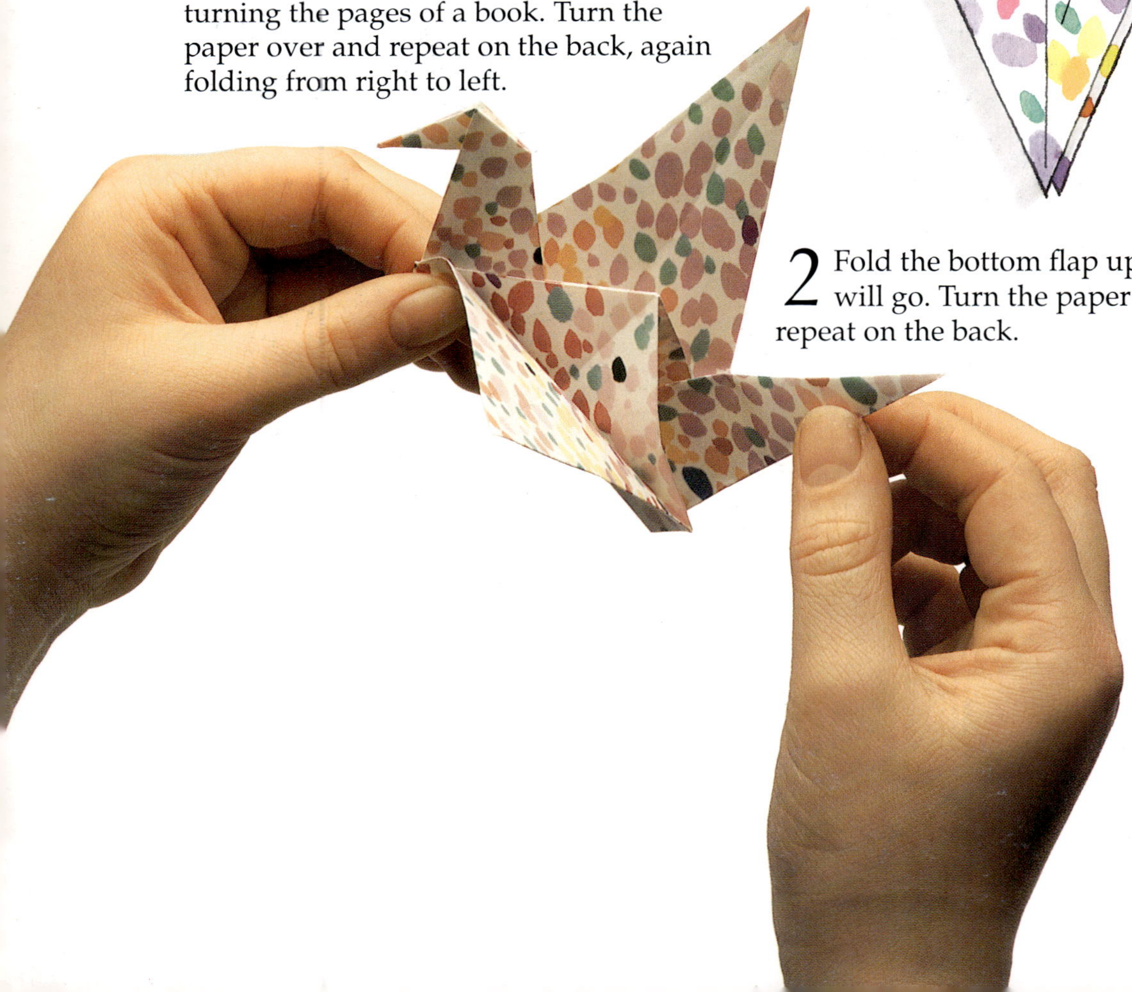

Rocket

This rocket can stand by itself, or it can be glued to stationery, notecards and posters. This makes it suitable as a theme for a party. Make rockets in one size for invitations or as party favours and in a very large size for hanging decorations. Origami paper, stationery and giftwrap are suitable, but silver foil giftwrap is more dramatic. The rocket begins with the waterbomb base.

You will need:
A paper square

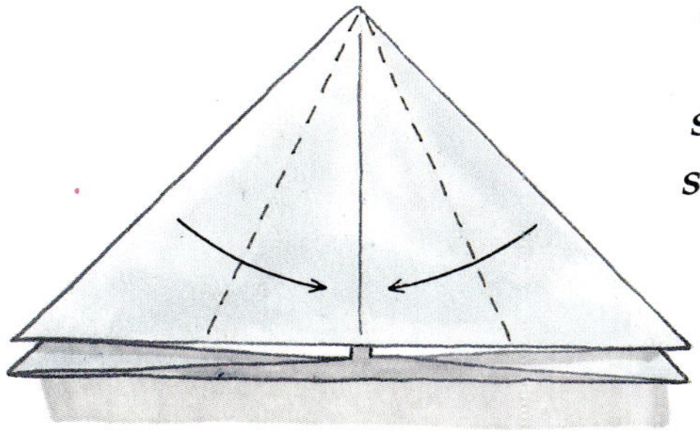

1 Follow steps 1 to 3 for the fruit (page 80). The paper now looks like this. Fold the outer *edges* of both front flaps to the middle. Turn the paper over and repeat on the back.

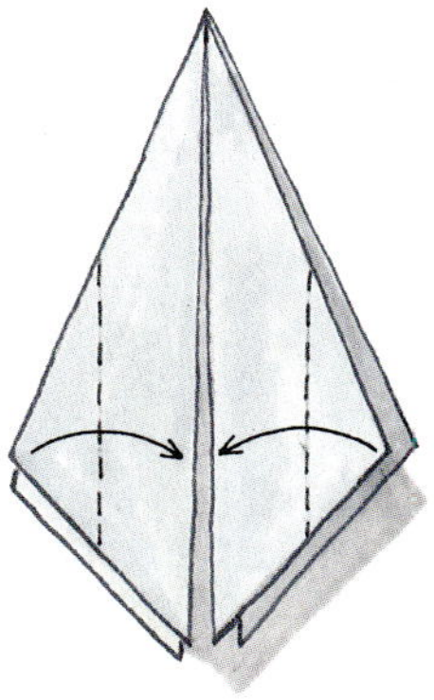

2 Fold the outer corners to the middle. Turn the paper over and repeat on the back.

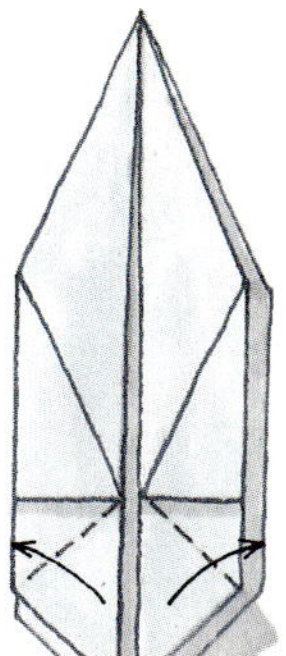

3 Fold the bottom points out. Repeat on the back.

4 Poke your finger into the rocket and gently open it. It will stand, ready for countdown.

Invitations

For gluing on party invitations and other cards, omit step 4 of the instructions and leave the rocket flat.

Dinosaur

With origami dinosaurs you can populate prehistoric landscapes large and small. Whether you prefer to glue small dinosaurs on a piece of sugar (construction) paper or make big standing dinosaurs depends only on the size of the square you use at the beginning. The folding pattern is the same.

You will need:
A square of paper, 15cm (6in) or larger

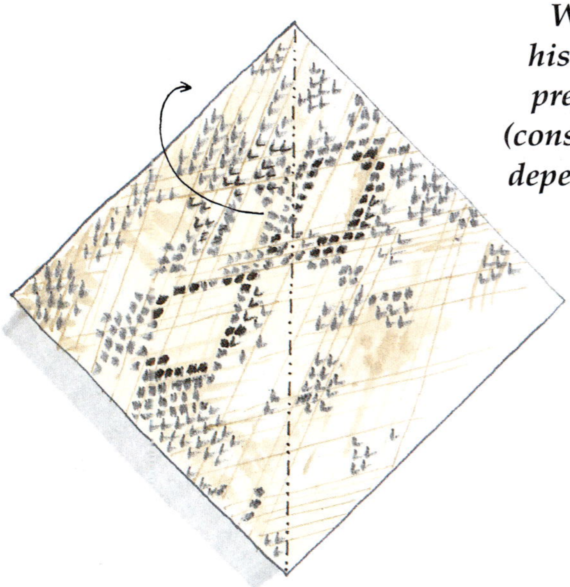

1 With the coloured side up, mountain fold the square on the diagonal. Unfold.

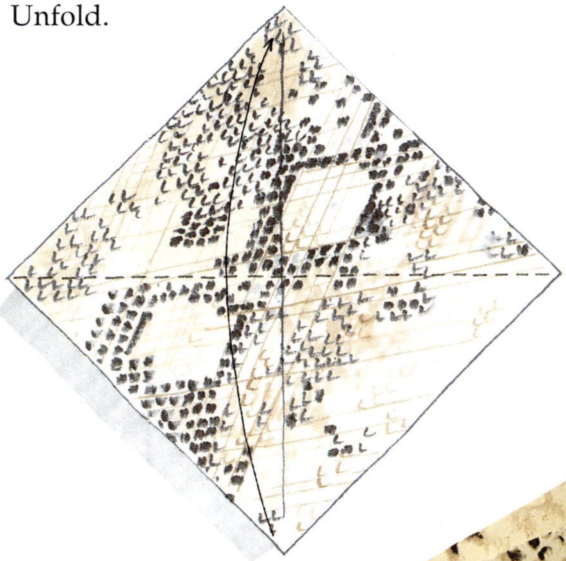

2 Valley fold the other diagonal. Do not unfold.

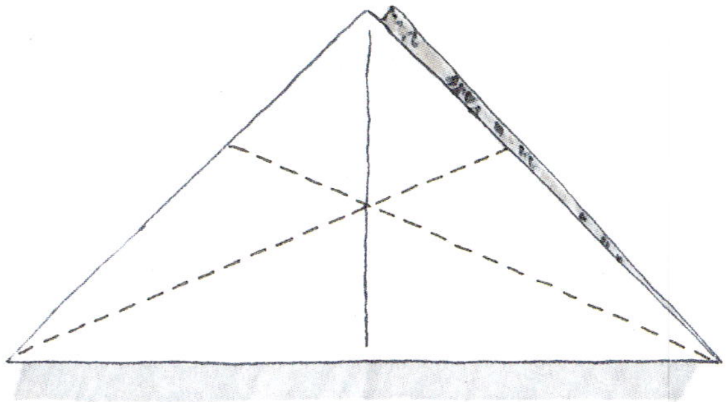

3 Fold the two side edges of the front layer of paper to the bottom edge. Unfold each time. Turn the paper over and repeat on the back.

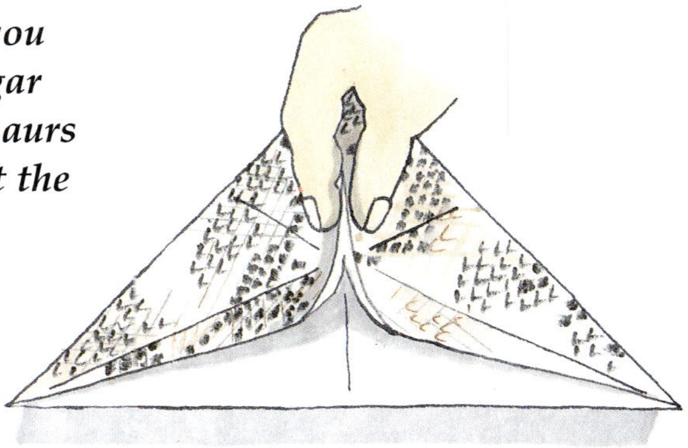

4 Pinch the top corner of the front layer of paper between your thumb and forefinger to make the short vertical crease AB. Keep holding and push down to let the paper settle into the two slanted creases made before. Flatten the pinched corner to the left. Repeat on the back, but flatten the pinched corner to the right.

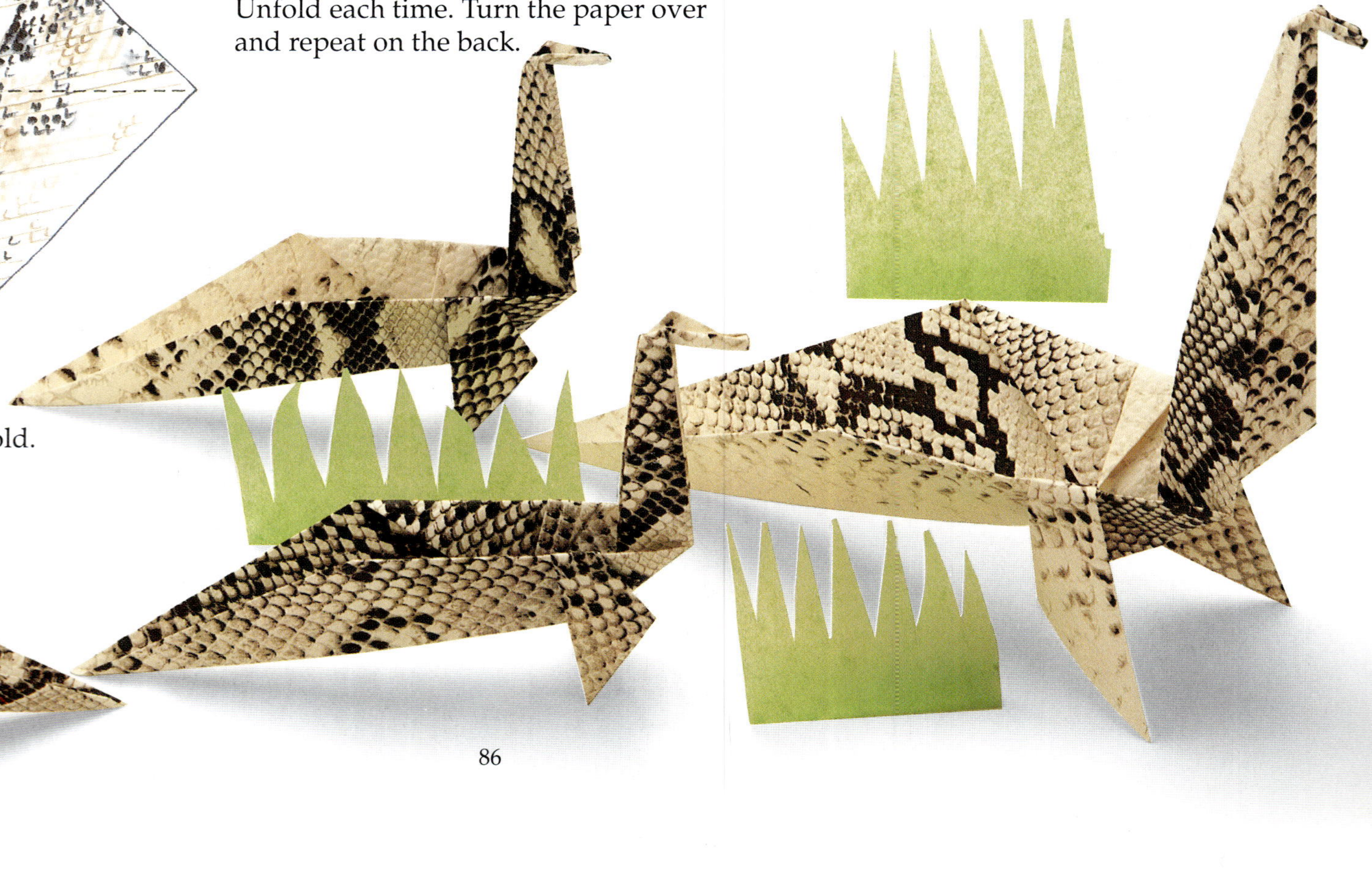

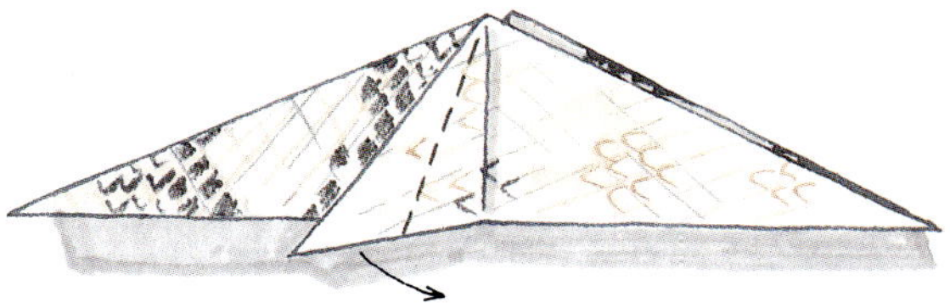

5 Fold over as shown to make the leg. Repeat on the back.

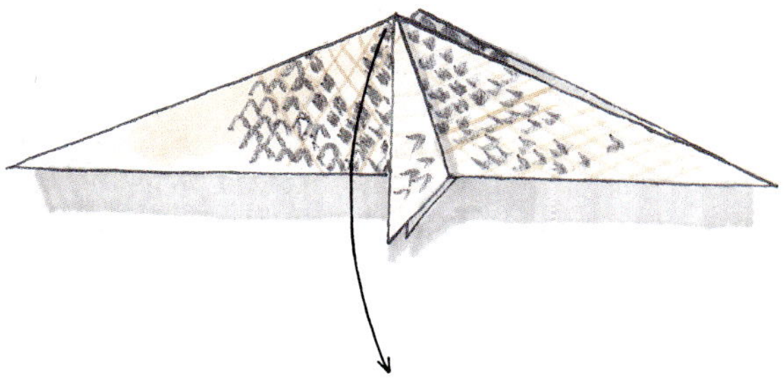

6 Open the paper flat. The legs are underneath on the right.

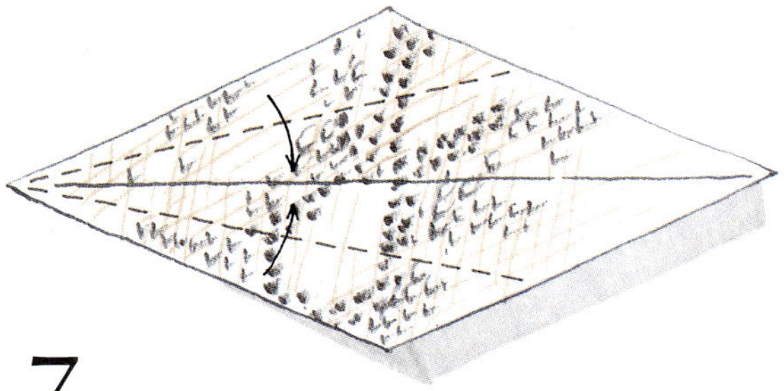

7 Fold the two edges to the middle.

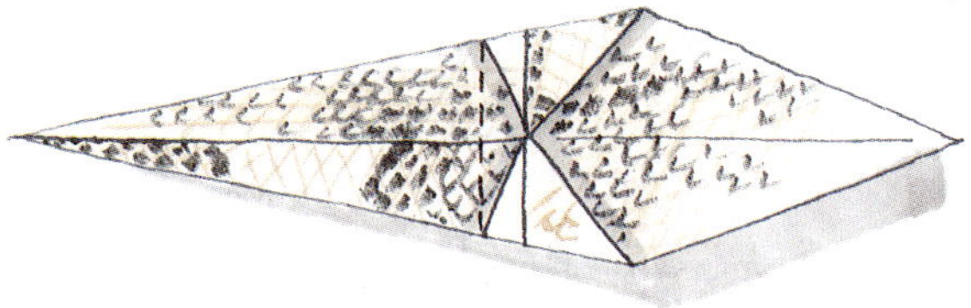

8 Form the neck with a valley fold.

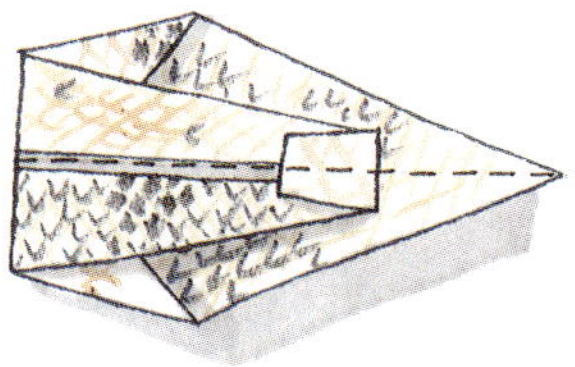

9 Then form the head with two more valley folds.

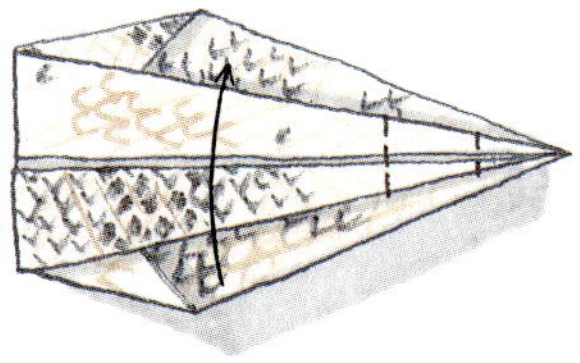

10 Valley fold the paper in half lengthwise. The legs will swing out.

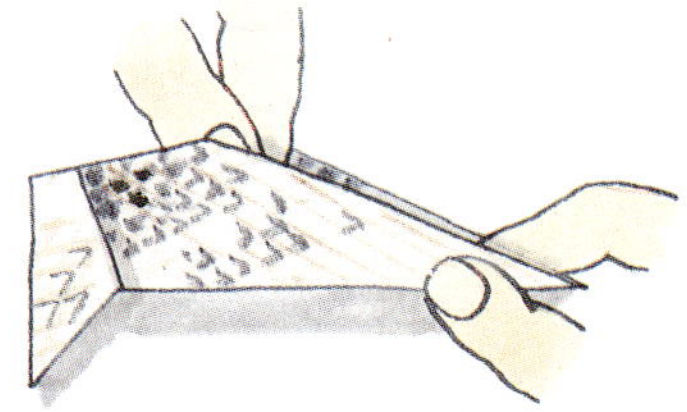

11 Let the paper open slightly. Reach inside and lift up the neck until it is almost vertical. To make it stay in place, crease the short edge at the front sharply.

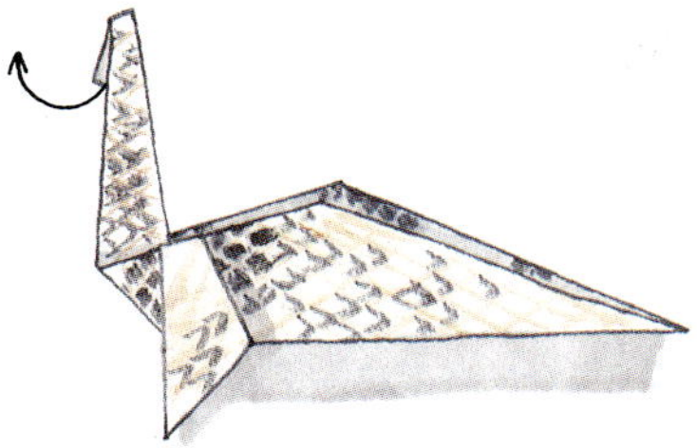

12 Pull the head forward. Crease sharply at the back of the head to make it stay in place.

Loch Ness Monster 1

The Loch Ness Monster is composed of a string of squares, which are folded much like the dinosaur. These squares are taped together after they are folded. Method 2 is more challenging, because the monster is folded from one long strip, according to the classic rules of origami which eschew taping. Both methods are given here. It is best if you fold the dinosaur a few times before making the Loch Ness Monster.

You will need:

Three 10cm (4in) origami squares
Sticky tape

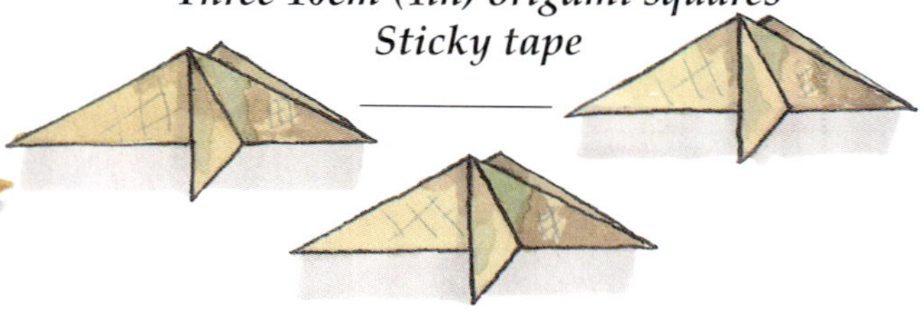

1 Fold the squares like the dinosaur from steps 1 to 5. The papers now look like the drawing for step 6 of the dinosaur.

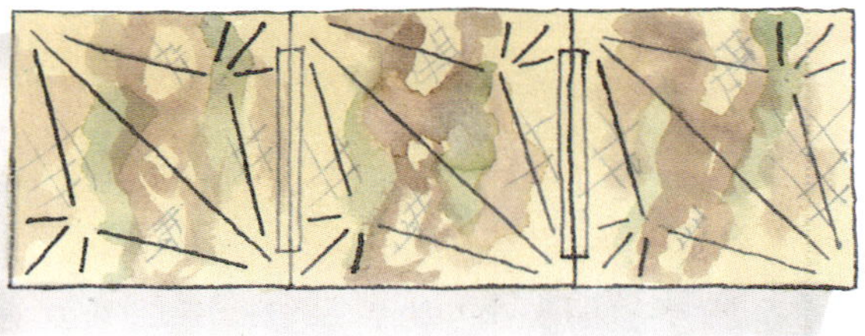

2 Unfold the papers flat. Line them up next to each other, all facing the same way. Tape the edges together. If you tape underneath, it will not show.

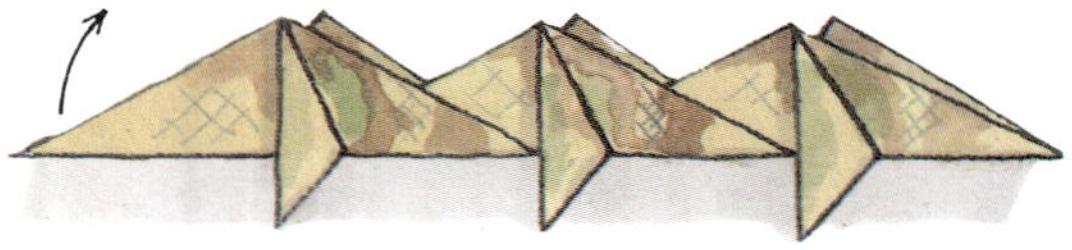

3 Refold all the squares.

4 Make the neck and head at the front end by following steps 8 to 12 of the dinosaur.

Loch Ness Monster 2

This is the real challenge. The instructions assume that you know how to fold the dinosaur. It may also help to have folded Nessie with Method 1, because you will then have a completed model to look at.

You will need:
A strip of paper 10cm by 30cm (4in by 12in)

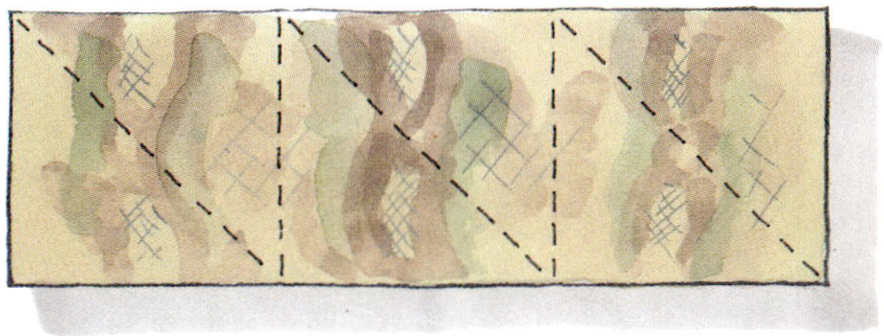

1 If the paper is coloured on one side only, begin with the white side up. Valley fold the strip as shown.

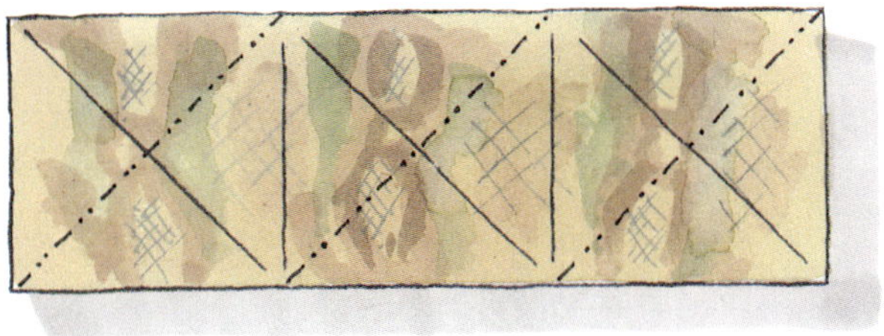

2 Mountain fold as shown.

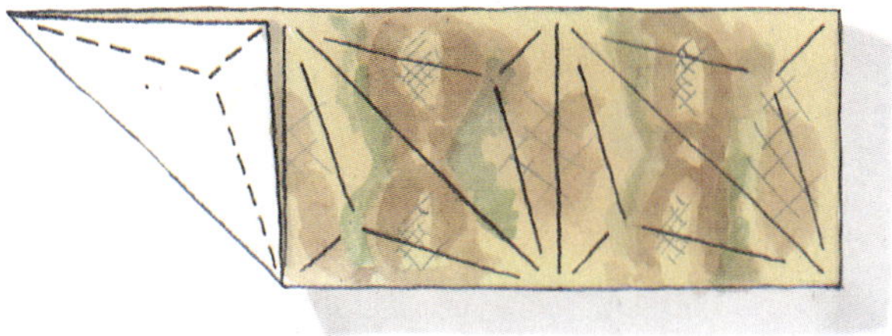

3 Fold steps 3 and 4 of the dinosaur all along the strip. You will be dealing with extra layers of paper as you perform some of the steps. Keep in mind that you want to fold a dinosaur on each square.

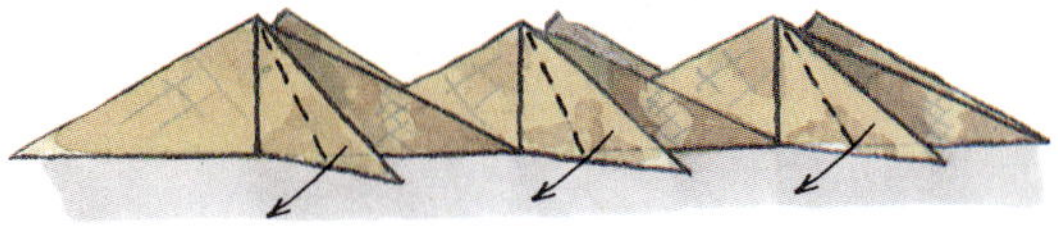

4 Narrow the triangles for the feet (step 5 of the dinosaur).

5 Follow steps 8 to 12 of the dinosaur.

A Monstrous Nessie

You can make a long Loch Ness Monster by adding as many squares as you like. The illustration shows one with 50 feet (25 each side) folded from a piece of paper approximately 12cm by 300cm (5in by 125in). The first one I ever made had a hundred feet and I called it a centipede.

Zig-Zag Graphics

Geometrics have great appeal for many people. If you are among them you may enjoy making zig-zag graphics. They are based on a grid creased on high quality paper. Students in art and architecture schools often work with zig-zag type constructions to encourage creative experiments. They usually use craft knives to score the creases, but with the zig-zag described here you do not have to measure or score the paper once you have the initial square. It is all done by folding.

Folding a zig-zag is quite challenging. If it is not for you then perhaps you can look on it as you would a recipe in a cookbook: you are pleased to know about it but have no desire to prepare it yourself.

You will need:

A square of high quality bond paper or good quality giftwrap

1 Fold the paper into eight sections. Because of the thickness of the paper, a good method is to fold the paper in half, fold it in half once more, then bring both outer edges to the middle crease. Sharpen all the creases by folding them first to the front and then to the back (mountain and valley folds). Open the paper flat.

Zig-Zag Sculpture

A paper sculpture which has been standing in our home for several years has caused the most surprised comments by many visitors. I folded a large piece of paper as suggested in the size and shape variation. I rolled it into a column and taped the edges together on the inside.

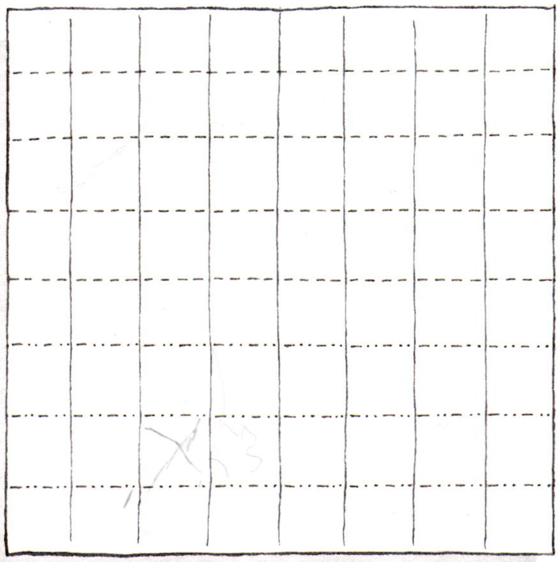

2 Repeat step 1 across the paper, at right angles to the first creases.

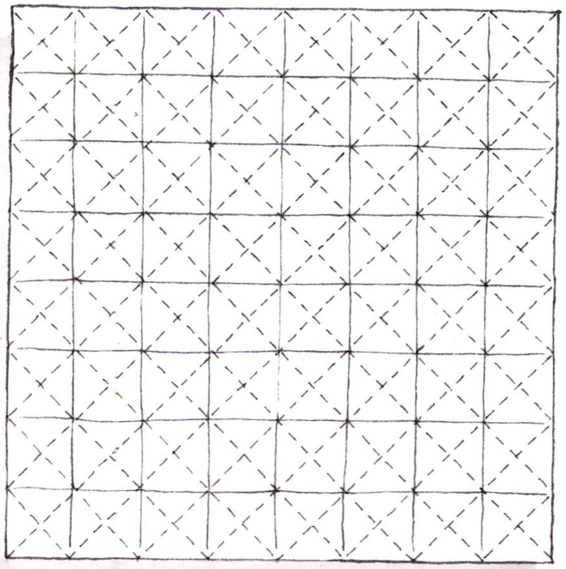

3 Crease the paper diagonally, in both directions through all the squares. Again sharpen each crease by folding it to the front and then to the back.

4 Pleat the paper like a fan, up and down the creases made in step 1 (alternate mountain and valley folds).

5 Now you have to get your piece of paper to look like that shown below. Do it row by row. The first one is simple and should look like the top of the cactus on page 77 when you have done it. Make sure that the top left-hand corner is exactly the same as that shown.

6 Now comes the tricky bit. The second and third rows are done together and you have to get the second row to slope back and the third row to slope forward. They will more or less pop into shape. The fourth and fifth rows are done exactly the same as the second and third rows, and so on down the sheet of paper.

Varying the Size and Shape

Once you have mastered the popping technique you can work on variations. Try a piece of paper 30cm by 20cm (12in by 8in). Make the first creases parallel to the short side. Then make a corner crease. Let these creases guide you into making the rest of the creases in steps 2 and 3. Note: the pleating in step 5 is made parallel to the short edge.

Colours

To my mind white paper is most satisfactory for making zig-zags, because the shadows show up most dramatically as variations of grey. Yet zig-zags made from coloured paper appeal to many people. The illustration shows a zig-zag made from a striped piece of giftwrap, which creates a most puzzling effect. I have been asked whether I painted the paper or whether I laboriously cut the individual sections of paper.

Framing

Because of the depth of a folded zig-zag, shadow box framing is required. As this can be quite costly, I adapt inexpensive plastic box frames, sold in photography shops. Glue a zig-zag to the inner box, then slide the plastic covering on top as far as possible. Tape the two parts together with sticky tape at all four corners.

You can cover the inner box with a piece of coloured paper before gluing on the zig-zag. I have achieved very pleasing results by folding a zig-zag from gold foil giftwrap and placing it on a royal blue or black background.

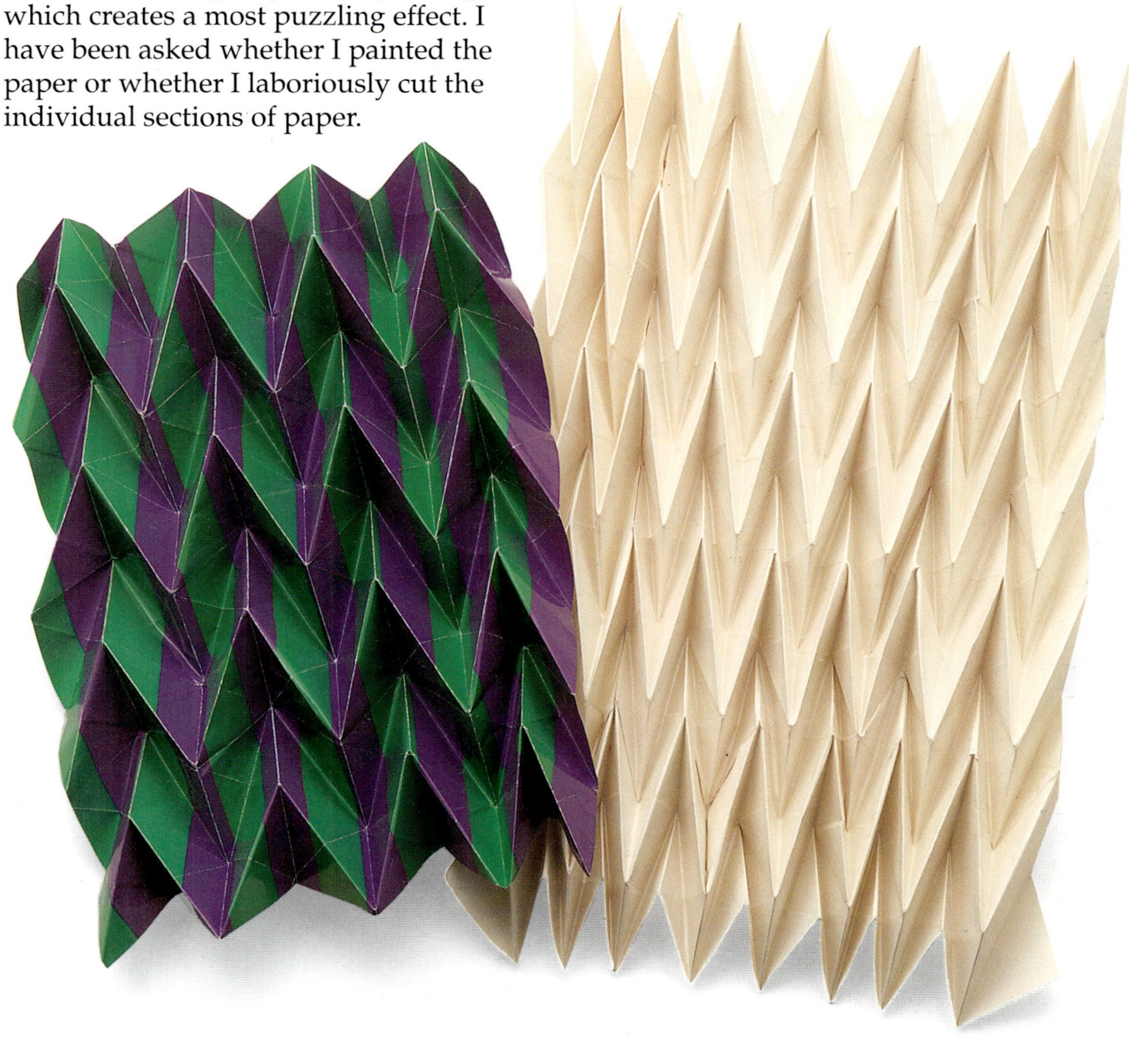

Pop-Ups and Constructions

Everybody loves a surprise and the projects in this section present unexpected effects. Hearts pop out of an ordinary-looking greetings card and a cat stands ready to keep you company.

This section also includes a triple-view picture, sometimes called kinetic art. Whichever it is called, the picture remains stationary, but the designs change as the viewer moves around. The first triple-view picture I saw was probably over a hundred years old. It showed three faces of local dignitaries. The next triple-view picture I saw was presented as kinetic art. It was a painting by the contemporary artist Avram who uses the technique extensively. I have developed a fairly simple method to produce triple-view pictures using ordinary art papers.

Flower Giftwrap for Bottles

This is my favourite way to wrap bottles, because nothing could be simpler, yet produce such a dramatic effect. You can use two sheets of tissue paper of the same colour, or two different, compatible colours.

You will need:

2 sheets of tissue paper
Sticky tape, ribbon, scissors

1 Place the two sheets on top of each other. Place the bottle near one of the short edges. Roll it up inside the whole length of the paper.

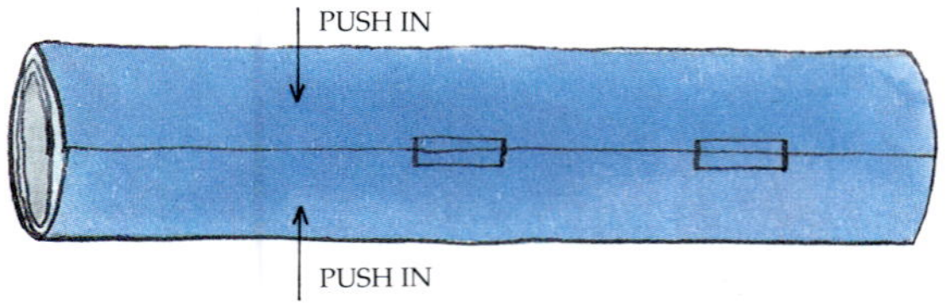

2 Secure with two or three pieces of sticky tape. Fold the small amount of spare paper under the bottom and tape with sticky tape. Bunch the paper around the bottom of the neck of the bottle.

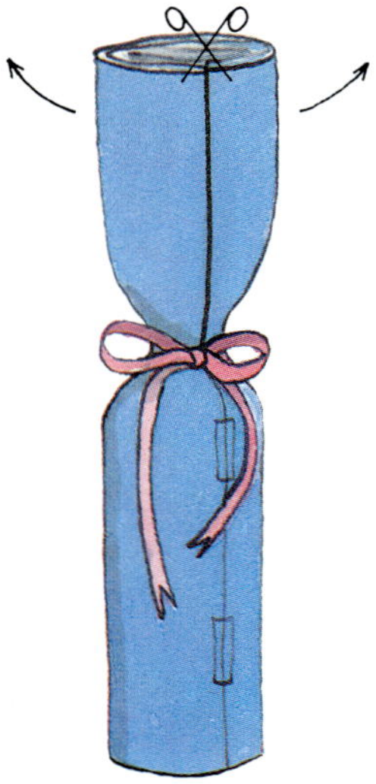

3 Wind the ribbon tightly round the bottom of the neck and tie the ends in a bow. Slit all the layers of paper from the top edge to the ribboned neck.

4 Beginning with the outer layer, pull the paper down, twisting the first layer to one side then the next layer to the other side to form a flower.

Smaller Bottles

For smaller bottles of spices, jams or cosmetics, use paper about 12cm (5in) wider than the height of the bottle.

Valentine Pop-Up

Everyone loves receiving a Valentine card and a handmade one becomes especially meaningful. This one uses the hearts design from the wall frieze on page 16.

You will need:

A 15cm (6in) square of red paper
Blank greeting card and envelope
Pencil, scissors, glue

1 Follow steps 1 to 4 of the directions for cutting the hearts design on page 16.

2 With the red side of the paper up, you will see that two opposite hearts are crossed by mountain folds. Place the mountain folds directly on the middle crease of the greetings card. This provides the pop-up mechanism.

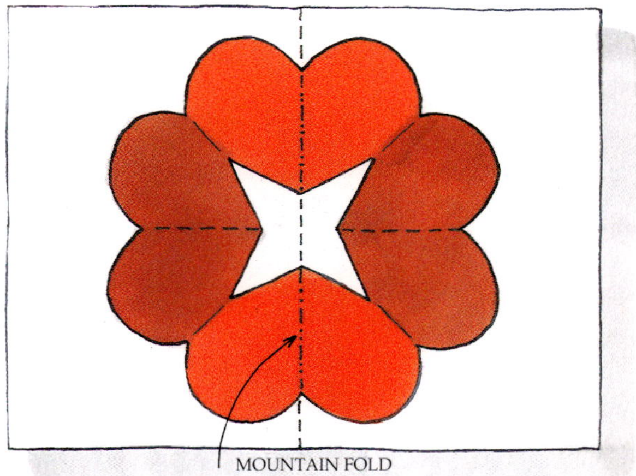

3 Glue down the two hearts on the right and left (shown darker in the illustration). Do not glue down the top and bottom hearts. Close the card.

4 The hearts pop up when the card is opened. The design suggests the message 'You are the Star of my Heart'. You can write it on the front of the card or, in small letters, inside the cutout star. You can also decorate the outside of the card with smaller cutout hearts.

Kangaroo Birth Announcement

Kangaroo mother with baby in her pouch will bring a smile to anyone's face. What a novel way to send a birth announcement or birth congratulations!

You will need:

A piece of brown sugar (construction) paper or similar weight for Mother Kangaroo
A small piece of yellow paper for Baby Kangaroo
A small piece of giftwrap paper for the heart-shaped pouch
Tracing paper or photocopy (see below)
Pencil, felt-tip pen, stapler, scissors, glue

1 Trace or photocopy the outlines and markings for Mother Kangaroo, Baby Kangaroo and the heart-shaped pouch.

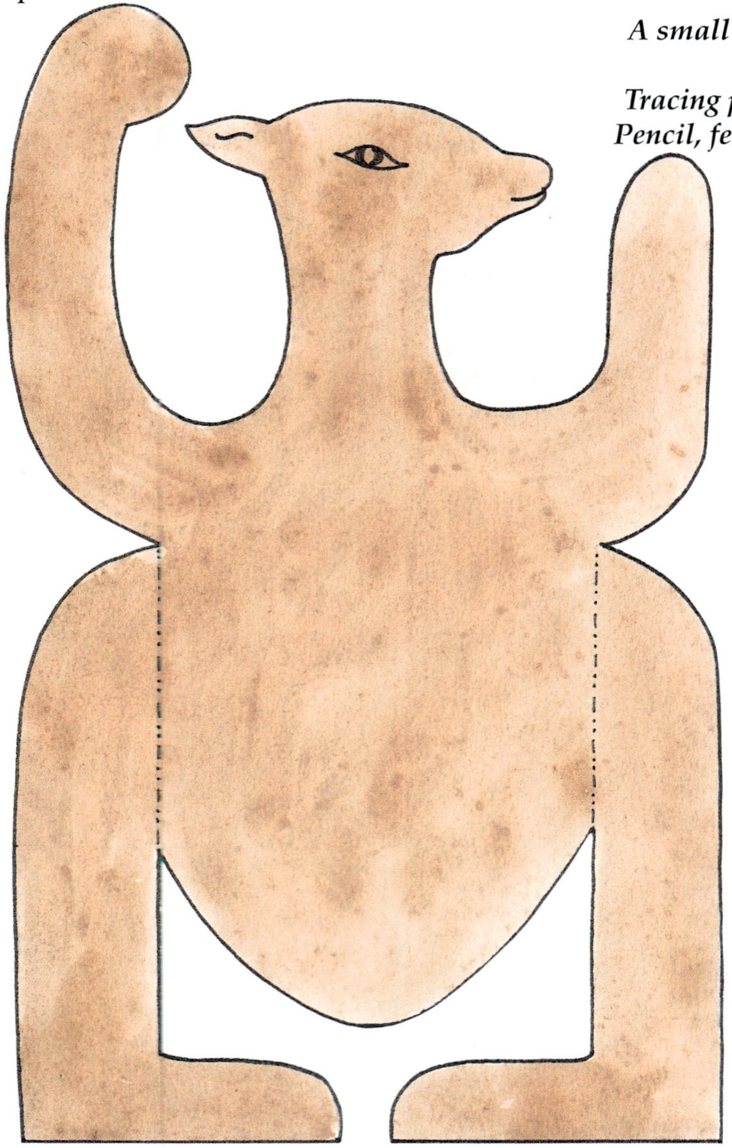

ACTUAL SIZE

2 Place the tracing or photocopy of Mother Kangaroo on the brown paper. Staple them together outside the picture area. Cut out Mother Kangaroo through both layers. Copy the face markings in felt-tip pen and the fold lines in pencil.

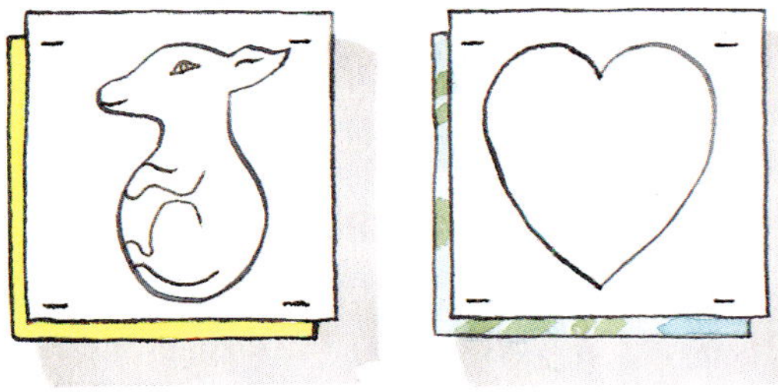

3 Place the tracing or photocopy of Baby Kangaroo on the yellow paper. Cut through both layers. Do the same with the heart-shaped pouch and the giftwrap paper. Copy Baby Kangaroo's face in felt-tip pen.

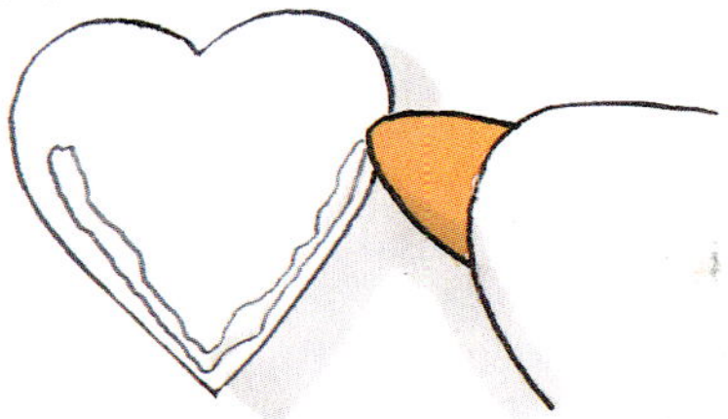

4 Glue the pouch on Mother Kangaroo but at the sides and bottom only, leaving the top open. Insert Baby Kangaroo into the pouch.

5 Mountain fold Mother's legs to the back so the card will stand up.

6 Finally write the birth announcement or greeting on the back of the card. Alternatively, for a birth announcement you could make small cards giving the baby's name and details and stick it to the back of Mother Kangaroo with double-sided sticky tape or fold it small enough to tuck into the pouch.

A Batch of Kangaroos

If you and your family are ambitious you can make a batch for birth announcements ahead of time. When the baby arrives prepare small cards with the name and other details.

Giant Kangaroo

You can make an oversize card or poster by enlarging the design and cutting it from Ingres or Canson Mi-teinte papers (see page 8).

Angel

What could be simpler than this angel, which you can hang on a Christmas tree or stand on the mantelpiece? If possible use duo-coloured paper to give contrasting colours for the body and the wings of the angel. Two pieces of foil giftwrap glued together is particularly effective and you can use glitter, stars and other stickers to decorate the finished angel.

1 Trace or photocopy the angel and its halo. Place the designs on top of the paper. Cut out through both papers on all the solid lines. With felt-tip pen copy the face markings.

2 Slide slit A into slit B behind the angel.

You will need:

Foil giftwrap paper
Tracing paper or photocopy (see below)
Felt-tip pen, scissors

3 Fold the arms to the front as shown by the dotted lines. Fold the hands up and glue them together. Glue on the halo.

Decorations

Glue on stickers, glitter, stars or gold ribbon. Or stick on foil paper or gummed paper cut into small geometric shapes.

HALO
B
A

Cylinder Characters

You can create all kinds of paper people when you roll a flat sheet into a cylinder. Draw or glue on some simple features and you can have elegant place cards for the dinner table, Christmas ornaments and other seasonal decorations. The instructions for the basic characters are followed by various examples. They show what you can make, depending on the extra materials you choose to add.

1 Roll the paper into a cylinder.

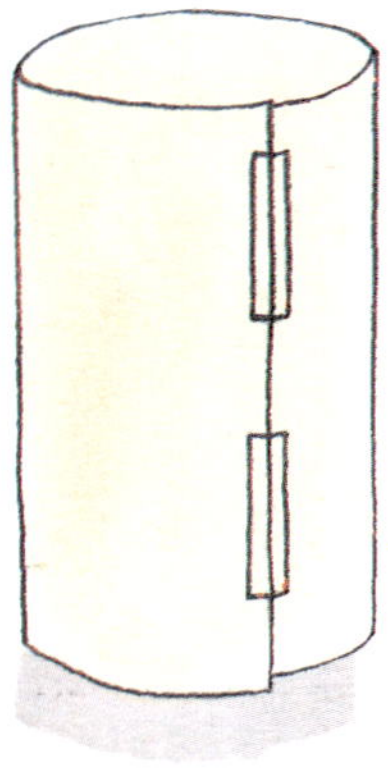

2 Overlap the edges and tape, glue or staple them together.

For table decorations you will need:

A piece of stiff paper 23cm by 13cm (9in by 5in) or half a sheet of sugar (construction) paper
Sticky tape, scissors, glue, stapler
Felt-tip pens and other extras (see below)

3 Choose one of the characters described and follow the instructions, or make up your own character.

Easter Rabbit

Cut the ears from the rest of the paper you used for the body and glue them inside the cylinder. Draw on the eyes and a triangular nose. Cut the whiskers from narrow strips of paper.

Santa Claus

Make the cylinder from red paper. Add a cone-shaped hat made from a semi-circle and glue on a cotton ball as a tassel. Glue on a white cotton beard. Glue on a paper belt with a buckle made from card.

Family

Make several bodies. For hair and beards, cut long paper strips and glue them on. If you like, they can be curled by rolling them over a pencil. Cut out and glue on paper lips, eyes and so on.

Whimsy

Combine some of the features shown in the examples. Cut out or fold paper hats (see page 73). Glue on cutout hearts, flowers, stars and other designs shown in the Mostly Cutting section of this book. Let yourself go with crazy extras.

Cylinder Giants

Place a large paper person in a corridor to show visitors where to go, or use several cylinder people as advertisements. For these bigger sizes, use thin cardboard cut as large as you require.

Wild Animals

The following wild animals demonstrate two simple ways in which paper can be turned into standing figures. The cat on pages 104–5 shows another way. They can be used as children's toys, party decorations and gifts. I suggest you use sugar paper or thin card. Giftwrap can be used but only if two sheets are glued together to make it strong enough. The first animal is the rhinoceros and is made with the single-fold method.

You will need:

Sugar (construction) paper, thin card or giftwrap glued double
Tracing paper or photocopy (see below)
Pencil, scissors, black felt-tip marker

1 Trace or photocopy the rhinoceros.

2 Fold a piece of paper or card in half. Place the rhinoceros on the paper with its back lined up on the folded edge.

3 Cut out the rhinoceros through all three layers. Draw on the eyes and ears.

Howling Coyote

The howling coyote is made in the same way as the rhinoceros except that the straight fold is vertical. Combine the coyote with the Blooming Cactus on page 77 for a desert setting.

Alligator

The alligator, like the rhinoceros, is made with the single-fold method. Cut out along the lines through all three layers, including the teeth. Bend the bottom row of the teeth down a little. Punch out the eye. This method can be used for making other kinds of animals whose head is on an even line with the back.

Elephant

The elephant is made with the slit-slit method. Slide the slits into each other to make it stand up. Elephants sometimes participate in Indian festivals, when their heads are elaborately decorated and they carry embroidered saddles for seating important personages. You can copy these decorations by gluing on confetti and other bits of paper.

Big Sizes

The animals can be made much larger. Most of the outlines are simple enough to be enlarged freehand. For giant animals a heavier card is needed, in which case the back line on the single-fold animals may have to be scored with a craft knife.

FOLDED EDGE
CREASE HERE
FOLDED EDGE
CUT 2
FOLDED EDGE

Your Favourite Cat

Your favourite cat can be made to stand by propping it up as with an easel. Glue on a photograph of your own cat's face to make it more personal.

You will need:
Thin card
Tracing paper or photocopy (see below)
Scissors, felt-tip pen, glue

1 Trace or photocopy the outlines of the cat and the stand. Place the design on top of the card and cut out through both layers.

2 Glue part of the stand to the back of the cat as shown, so it will not show from the front. Crease and bend the stand away from the body at a right angle.

3 Draw on the cat's face with a felt-tip pen, or glue on a photograph of your own cat's face.

A Family of Cats

You can make some kittens to go with your cat. Make another photocopy of the cat outline, but have it reduced to two thirds or half the size.

Greetings Card

Write your greeting on the back or on a separate piece of pretty paper. Make an envelope big enough to take the cat and greeting (see page 21).

Reindeer

The reindeer is made to stand by a combination of the single-fold and the slit-slit methods. You can use it on its own or with the pine tree (page 29).

You will need:

A sheet of plain brown or textured A4 paper
Tracing paper or photocopy (see below)
Pencil, scissors

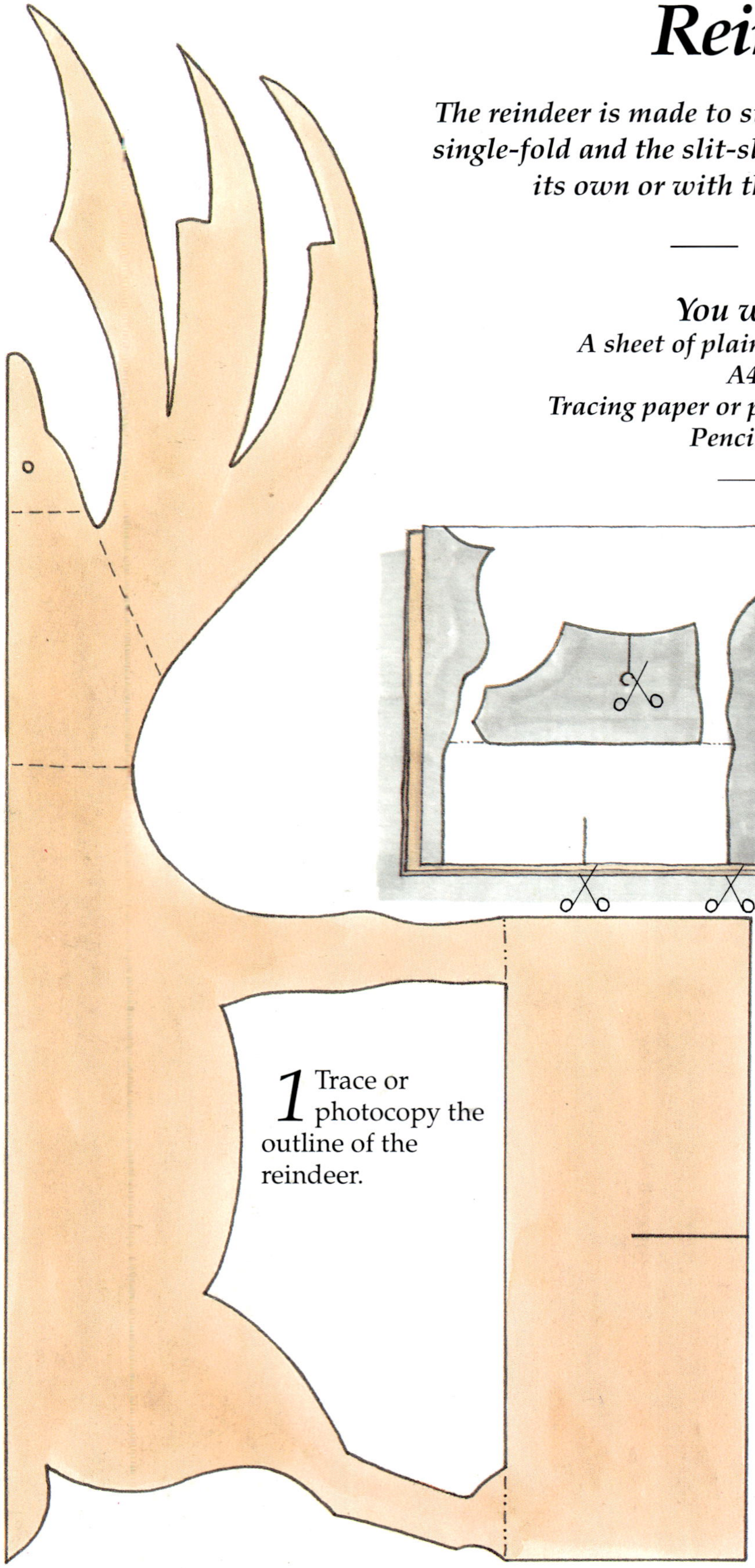

1 Trace or photocopy the outline of the reindeer.

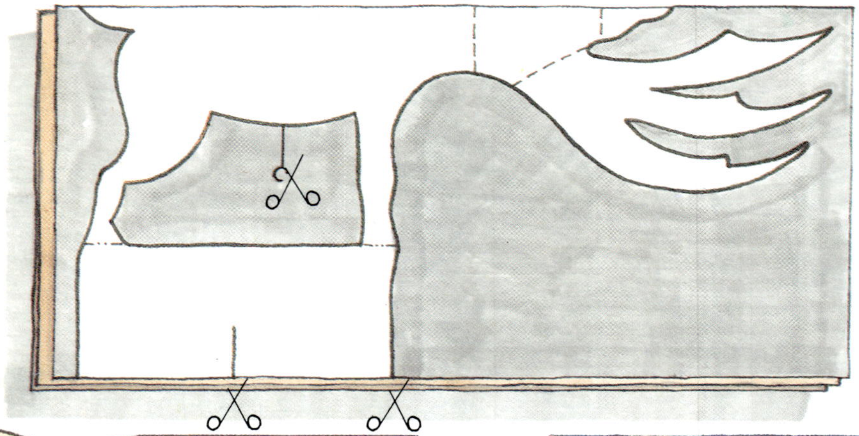

2 Fold a piece of paper in half lengthwise. Place the tracing or photocopy on the folded paper with the top of the reindeer on the folded edge. Secure the tracing or photocopy with paper clips or staples outside the cutting area. Cut through all three layers. The shaded areas fall off.

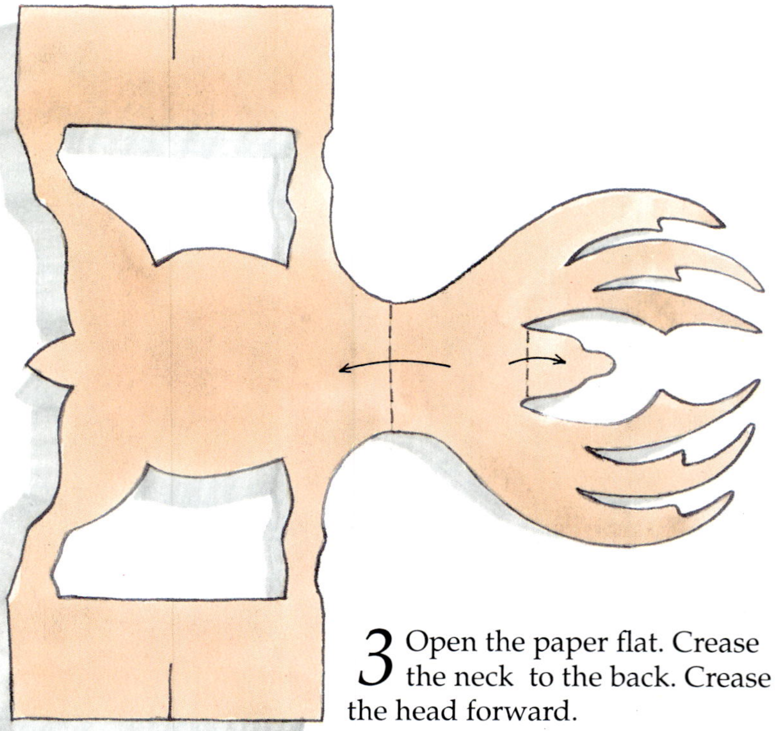

3 Open the paper flat. Crease the neck to the back. Crease the head forward.

Fastening
The shades can be held together by stapling, gluing or lacing with yarn.

Translucent Shades
Paper lampshades can be made translucent by brushing or sponging them with a half-and-half solution of boiled linseed oil and turpentine. Leave to dry for 15 minutes. Wipe off any excess with paper towels.

Decoration
Each flute can be ornamented in the following ways:

Slitting: Fold flute in half and cut parallel lines from the folded edge.

Cutouts: Cut out triangles, hearts or flower petals with a craft knife.

Appliqué: Cut geometric shapes, birds or flowers from tissue paper and glue them on. Layer the tissue paper unevenly for unusual effects.

Pinpricking: To perform this Victorian craft, pierce holes with a pin or fine nail in straight lines or decorative patterns.

Combining: These methods may be combined or may be used on alternate flutes.

Lining
For better diffusion of light, line the shade with slits and cutouts. Cut a piece of tracing paper the same size as each flute and include it when stapling the lampshade.

Different Shapes of Fluted Shade
Here are some ways of making different shapes of shade.

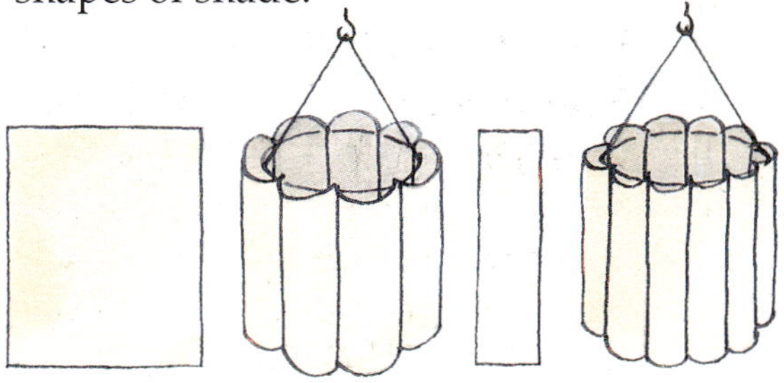

1 For a rectangular lampshade use six rectangles 15cm by 21cm (5½in by 8½in).

2 For a more fluted lampshade, use 12 rectangles 7½cm by 21cm (2¾in by 8½in).

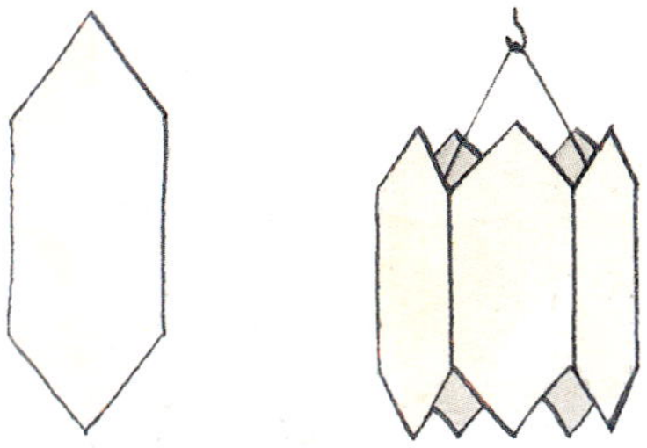

3 For a pointed lampshade, cut the top and bottom edges of the rectangles into points before joining the seams.

4 Slanting the sides of the rectangles will give a shade which is wider at the bottom than the top.

5 Combine slanted sides and pointed edges in any way you like!

Gift Bag

Popping a present into a pretty bag is more and more taking the place of customary gift wrapping. It's quicker, yet attractive, and especially handy for an odd-shaped present. Making the bag takes about as much time as regular wrapping. The bag is shaped by forming giftwrap around a box or a few books. Use good quality giftwrap or glue two thinner sheets together.

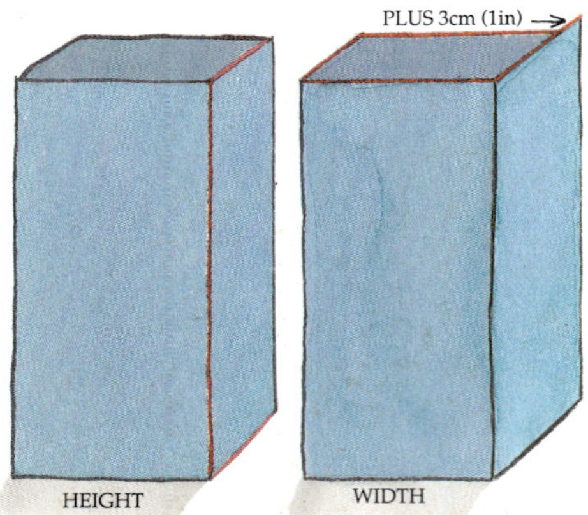

1 Use the box to measure the paper. The height will be the height of the box plus the width of the top and bottom. The width will be the width of the front, side, back and side, plus 3cm (1in) for extra overlap.

2 Fold down a long edge the same width as the top of the box.

You will need:

Giftwrap
¾metre (¾yd) cord or ribbon from stationery or material shop
Cereal box or other box
Sticky tape or glue, ruler, pencil, scissors, paper punch

3 Place the box on top of the white side of the paper. Wrap the paper around it letting it meet in the middle.

4 Tape or glue the edges together. Line up the top of the box with the folded edge.

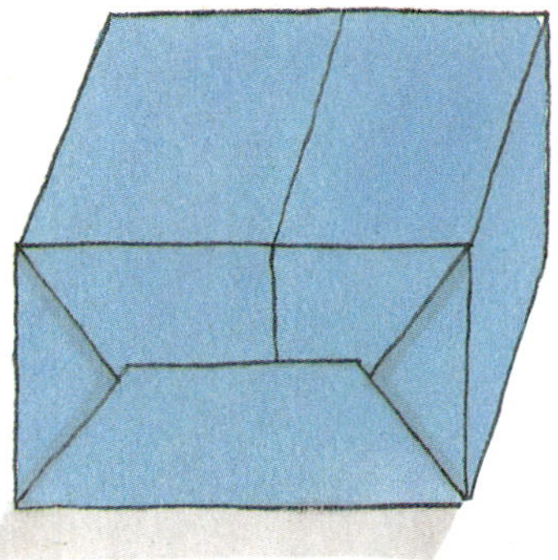

5 Wrap the bottom of the box as you would wrap a normal gift box. Glue or tape it closed. Remove the box.

6 Punch holes 2cm (¾in) from the top edge of the bag, two in front and two on the back, the same space apart.

7 Cut two pieces of cord 32cm (13in) approximately. Guide the cord through the holes. Double-knot all the ends of the cord inside the bag.

8 If you like you can put a piece of tissue paper loosely crushed into the top of the bag to cover the gift.

Variations

Instead of making two handles, guide a length of cord through the front, in and out the back and through the front again. Tie the ends into a bow.

To reinforce the bottom, cut a piece of card a little smaller than the bottom of the bag and put it in.

To fold the bag for storage, crease the middle of the sides. Push in the base of the sides to flatten the bottom of the bag against the back.

Luminarias

Luminarias are outdoor party lights that are made of nothing more than votive candles set in a bed of sand inside a paper bag. They are based on Spanish and Indian traditions and may be seen in parts of the United States during the Christmas season, when they line paths and drives, giving off a soft, flickering glow. They can be used at any time of the year and are particularly nice for a summer garden party.

You will need:

Small gift bags, approximately
15cm (10in) high
Paper punch, scissors
Votive candles or nightlights, sand or soil

Caution: Luminarias must only be used outside and under adult supervision. Place away from shrubbery and other things. The sand in the bottom of the bag extinguishes the flame when the candle burns down.

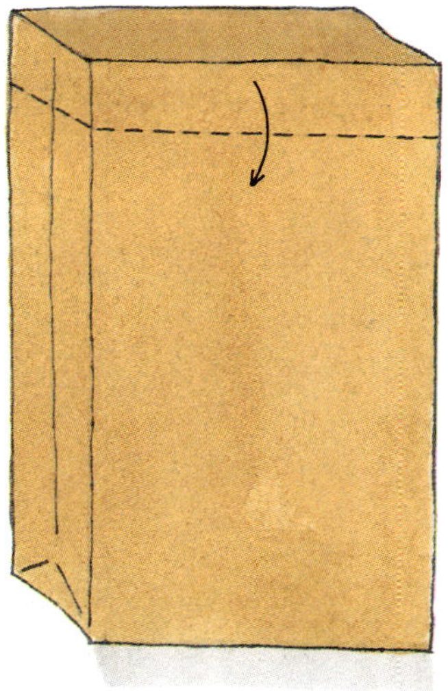

1 Turn down 4cm (1½in) at the top of the bag.

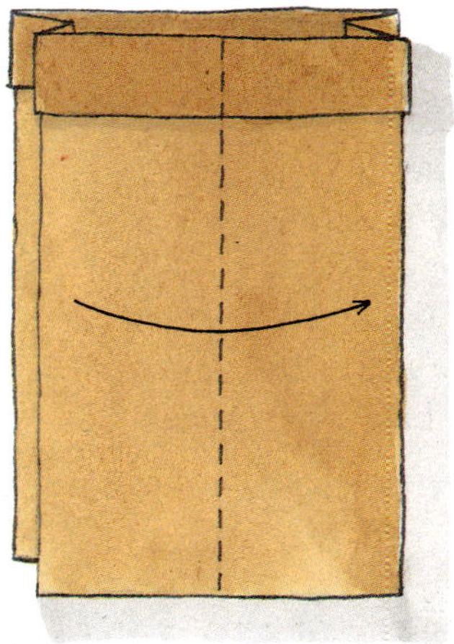

2 Fold the bag in half.

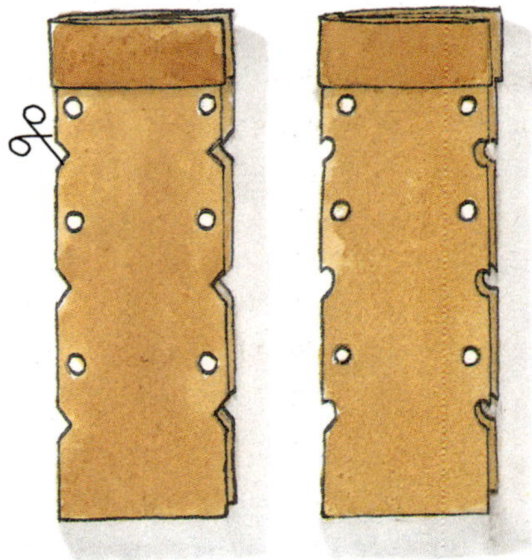

3 On the long edges cut out small shapes and punch holes.

4 Fill the bag with 5cm (2in) of sand or soil. Firmly set the votive candle upright into the sand.

Papermaking

In this section you will be introduced to a remarkable, yet fast process for making your own paper, beginning with flaky raw materials and ending up with a sheet. Later you can find out how to colour and decorate either your own handmade sheets or different kinds of bought paper by dip-dyeing and paste patterns.

Handmade paper has only been recognized as an art material for about twenty years. Until that time paper served as a support for printing and illustrations but now, in addition, it has become the medium itself. Artists have developed new techniques: casting in moulds, shaping into bas reliefs and three-dimensional sculptures, dyeing and combining with other materials into multi-media effects.

In keeping with the spirit of Made With Paper *the directions introduce you to simple processes resulting in fun papers for unusual, individual and stylish notecards, photocards, wallets, jewelry, giftwraps and other things. You can even apply some of the cutting and folding ideas shown in other parts of the book. These processes inspire almost everyone to experiment and explore all kinds of possibilities.*

Basic Papermaking by Hand

Among the many crafts which I have practised, papermaking seems to be the most surprising fun for all ages, because new and different results appear every few minutes.

I am introducing a new method, which allows you to start working with little preparation and using only supplies available from your local shops. Papers made with this simplified method result in textured, earthy sheets with a pronounced deckle edge, rather than the flat, straight-edged sheets made by machine. They are suitable for turning into unique decorations on greetings cards, stationery, gifts, knick-knacks or wherever else you would like to see a handcrafted effect.

The basic process for making paper involves dispersing pulp on a screen, where it forms a sheet. Customarily the screen is held between two wooden frames and this combination is called a mould. The mould can be bought ready-made from some art supply stores or can be made at home using wood. But I have discovered that a satisfactory mould can be made easily from two disposable aluminium baking pans in much less time.

After making the mould, you will discover how to make sheets of paper from facial tissues. Stationery, wrapping and other papers may be recycled with equally good results. Of course, you will want to use the sheets for practical purposes and you will find many suggestions to help you.

When two or three people work together they usually inspire each other with experimental suggestions: let's recycle this hot pink advertisement; let's sprinkle in some green vegetable leaves; let's try a tiny sieve for a mould. I think you will be pleased with the unexpected outcomes of this delightful activity.

Making a Mould

A mould is the most important piece of equipment required for making paper.

You will need:

Two aluminium baking pans, rectangular or square and 20 to 23cm across (8 to 9 in)
½ metre (½ yard) stiff nylon netting from material shops or pinpoint screening sold at hardware stores
Scissors, two spring-type clothespegs

1 Cut out the centre of both pans, leaving a 1cm (½ in) edge all around. It is best to pierce a hole in the middle of each pan and cut towards the corners as shown in the drawing. Do not cut all the way into the corners. **Caution**: The edges may be sharp!

2 Cut a piece of netting material large enough to cover the bottom of the baking pan and all four sides amply. Or cut a piece of pinpoint screening the same size as the bottom of the pan.

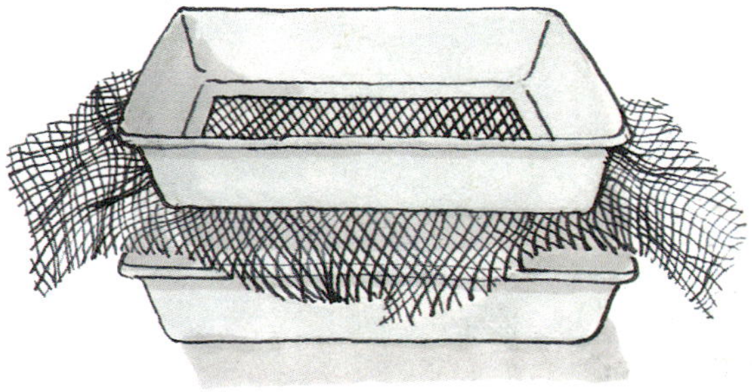

OR

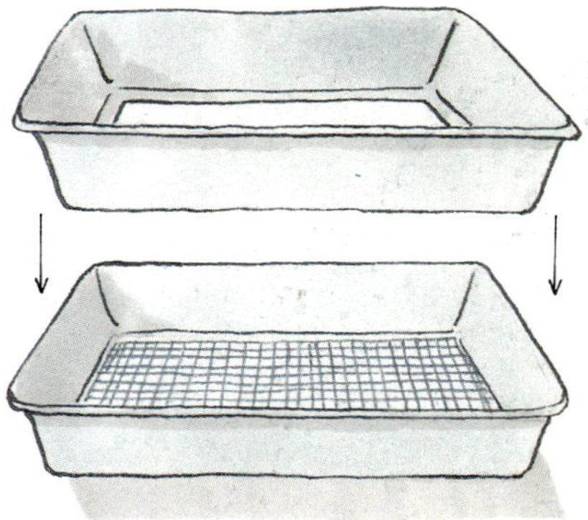

3 Sandwich the netting between the two pans. Make sure the material is stretched tightly. If the pinpoint screen does not lie flat, cut narrow slivers off the edges to make it fit.

4 Clip the pans together with the clothespegs.

Making the Pulp

This is the most simple and basic way of making paper. The kitchen is the best place to work, because a lot of water is needed to make paper.

1 Tear the tissues into approximately 2cm (1in) squares and put in the blender.

2 Add 750ml (three 8oz cups) of warm water.

3 Blend the tissues and water together until they form a soupy mixture. This takes about 2 minutes. (Do not fill the blender container more than two-thirds full.)

Pouring

4 Cut several pieces of blotting paper a bit larger than the mould. Set them aside.

5 Put the mould into the sink (with the plug in) or litter tray. Pour the well-stirred pulp over the whole of the screen. A snake-like movement helps to distribute it evenly. Look for bare spots and fill them with a little more pulp.

To make one sheet of paper you will need:

3 white facial tissues (do not use those marked 'wet strength')
Measuring jug
Blender
Several large pieces of blotting paper or synthetic dish cloths, such as J-cloths
Sink or large shallow container, such as a cat litter tray

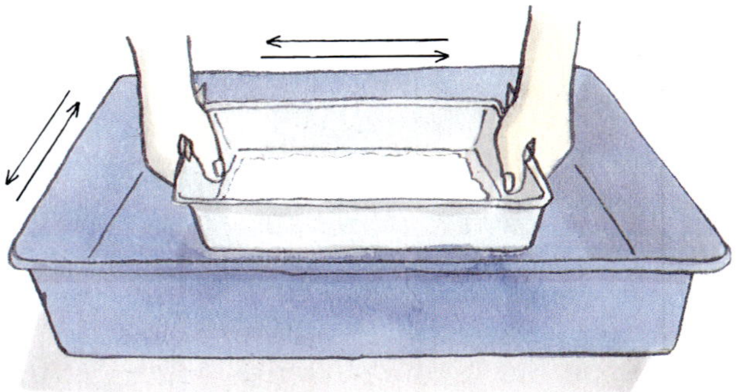

Stroking

6 Lift the mould a few centimetres off the bottom of the sink. Gently shake the mould from side to side and from front to back, twice. This action is called 'stroking' and strengthens the paper by locking the fibres together.

7 Hold the mould still for a while to let any left-over water drain back into the sink.

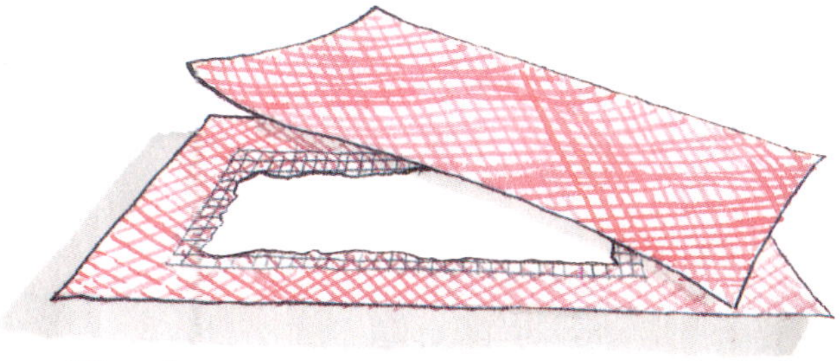

Drying

8 Remove the clothespegs from the mould. Take the screen with the paper on it and place it between two blotters.

9 Pat the blotter sandwich gently all over to squeeze out some of the excess water.

10 Use more blotters to soak up as much moisture as possible. The paper may cling to the screen or the blotter. Be careful not to disturb the paper; let it dry either on the screen or the blotter for a few hours, preferably in a warm place. When the paper is quite dry, peel it slowly off the screen or blotter. This completes the basic way of making paper.

Drying Cloths

You can never have too many drying cloths. I prefer viscose kitchen cloths, because they do not wrinkle. For other possibilities see page 121.

Disposal of pulp

Left-over pulp should be put in the dustbin and not poured down the sink, as it may clog the drains. Before disposing of the pulp, strain it through a kitchen sieve or the mould to squeeze out most of the water.

Variations on the Basic Method

Papermaking resembles cooking in that a basic recipe can be varied in many ways. Now that you know the basic papermaking recipe, you can experiment by changing the pulp, the shape of the mould and how much you make. If you want to write on your handmade paper it must be sized, either at the pulp stage or when it is dry.

Thinner Paper

The pouring method described so far produces a fairly thick, rough sheet of paper. For thinner paper follow these steps:

1 Set the mould into a sink or large plastic tray. Fill it with just enough water to cover the screen.

2 Pour the pulp over the screen with the usual snake-like movement, but use only enough pulp to cover the screen thinly and evenly.

3 Gently lift up the mould and shake it from side to side, from front to back.

4 Dry the paper in the usual way or couch it (see page 121).

Larger Amounts of Pulp

You can prepare larger amounts of pulp by using more facial tissues and water, but always keep the formula in the proportion one tissue to 250ml (1 cup) of water. Twelve tissues and 3 litres (12 cups) of water produces about four or five sheets.

Larger Sheets of Paper

The size of the paper is limited only by the size of the baking pans. To make a bigger sheet use larger disposable pans for the mould.

Other Pulp Ingredients

Other kinds of paper can be shredded into pulp. Try some of these:

- white or coloured paper napkins
- typing and computer paper
- new and used stationery
- lightweight paper carrier bags
- coloured tissue paper
- egg cartons (not plastic)

The procedure for making the pulp is the same as before, but different amounts of water are necessary for different kinds of papers. Aim for the same consistency as the pulp made from facial tissues. If the pulp is too watery, you can add more shredded paper. Most of these papers break down more easily when they are soaked in water from half an hour to overnight before pulping.

Some papers do not break down evenly, leaving lumps of pulp on the screen. If this happens, throw the pulp away and begin again with another kind of paper. Always rinse the screen clean.

Sizing

In order to write on handmade paper it must be sized to prevent the ink from streaking. A dried piece of paper can be sized by covering it with acrylic craft spray, or you can size the paper at the pulp stage.

Add one tablespoon of one of the following for every three facial tissues shredded into the pulp:

one teaspoon of white glue for every litre (four cups) of water

Or one tablespooon of instant liquid starch

Or mix a packet of unflavoured gelatin with 250ml (one cup) of hot water.

Varying the Quantities

Bear in mind that it is not necessary to adhere strictly to the recipes. In papermaking, quantities are flexible. For example, if the pulp contains too much water, it will just run through the screen. If you use too much colouring, the sheet will be darker.

Fancy Papers

Is it all right to snip sweet wrappers into the pulp? Perhaps, perhaps not. Sometimes the results are totally unexpected, but most outcomes are interesting and may lead to exciting results.

Coloured Papers

Coloured paper can be produced by adding colouring to the pulp. Try instant coffee, strong tea, food colours, powdered fabric dyes, tempera or acrylic paints. Dissolve these products in a little warm water first.

Natural, soft colours result from adding small pieces of plant leaves, vegetables, orange juice and other natural materials to the pulp before blending. Try cabbage, lettuce, onions, celery, and artichokes. Try too the leaves or petals of iris, gladiola, marigold, day lilies and other flowers. You may be surprised that only a few leaves or petals give out quite a lot of colour.

You could try making pulp from coloured papers. Newspapers result in grey paper, but what about a purple carrier bag?

Flecked and Spotted Paper

If you add shredded leaves, petals, confetti and other materials for about five seconds near the end of the pulping process, the pieces will not macerate completely and add flecks of colour.

Multi-Coloured Paper

Use pulp to paint a picture in your paper. Make pulp in two or more colours in separate cups or bowls. Pour the pulp, one colour at a time onto the mould in the shape you want.

More About Drying

Drying is an important part of papermaking which can be achieved in several different ways. Drying on the screen means that the screen cannot be used again immediately. Couching (pronounced kootching) is the professional way of drying paper. Post drying allows you to dry several sheets at once, but slowly. If you are in a hurry, I am suggesting several ways of speeding up the drying process.

Couching

In couching the damp paper is flipped off the screen onto a piece of absorbent fabric or blotting paper. This is the most difficult step in papermaking, because the paper wants to stick to the screen and may tear easily. Bear in mind that you are trying to squeeze most of the water out of the pulp.

1 Place the screen with the pulp between two blotters. Pat the sandwich until both blotters are very wet. Then replace with dry blotters.

2 Test one corner of the new sheet of paper to see if it will come away from the screen. If it sticks, continue to remove more water by using additional blotters, if necessary.

3 When the paper is ready to come away, place it on another blotter with the screen topmost. Take away the screen.

Post Drying

A whole pile of papers can be dried on top of each other. This is quicker and neater, because it avoids spreading papers everywhere while they are drying on blotters. Unfortunately you may have to wait a day or two before the papers are completely dry. You will need 30 to 40 blotters.

1 Couch one piece of paper as described above.

You will need:

Pulp spread evenly on the mould as described in the basic method
Lots of blotters
For post drying: *a wooden board or rolling pin, heavy books or bricks*

2 Put a dry blotter on top of the damp sheet and couch another sheet of paper on top.

3 Keep adding a blotter and a new sheet of paper until you have a pile of 12 sheets. This is called a 'post'.

4 Press out as much water as possible with your hands, or place a wooden board on top and press down hard. You can also use a rolling pin.

5 Place the whole pile on a dry towel and weigh it down with books or bricks until the paper is completely dry, which may take two days. The process can be speeded up by replacing the damp blotters with dry ones, but make sure that the new pieces of paper do not tear.

Flat Drying

This is a way of making paper with a silky smooth surface. Couch the paper on a flat surface, such as a formica kitchen counter, table top or flat oven tray. Remove the paper when it is really dry.

Oven Drying

A faster way of drying is to place the sheets of paper on their blotters in a cool oven (80ºC, 170ºF) for about 30 minutes .

Air Drying

When the sheets are semi-dry, they can be hung on a clothes line or over a shower curtain rod, or placed near hot air pipes. Prevent crinkling by hanging three or four sheets on top of each other.

Ironing

Ironing is a good way to dry a few sheets of paper when they first come off the screen or blotter. Ironing also helps to flatten crinkled, dry sheets. Use a blotter or press cloth (an old sheet or other smooth fabric) between the iron and the newly formed sheet of paper. Iron on low heat for about 3 to 5 minutes.

Blotters and Drying Cloths

These may be made from any materials which soak up water. Besides blotting paper, J-cloths, paper towels and white felt are recommended. Professional papermakers commonly use thick felt as their 'couching cloths'.
After use, any couching cloths must be dried without wrinkles. Wrinkled blotters may subsequently leave marks and should be discarded..
Always have a large supply of blotters or other couching cloths on hand.

Dip-Dyed Giftwraps

Dip-dyeing ordinary papers into your own unique sheets of giftwrap is a truly spectacular process. This adaptation of traditional fabric dyeing methods offers the thrill of quick results. After pleating paper in various ways, it is dipped into dye baths. Beautiful patterns emerge when the paper is unfolded and dried.

1 For your first attempt use half a sheet of tissue paper, which is easier to handle than a full sheet. Fan-pleat it parallel to a short edge into 3cm (1½in) wide strips.

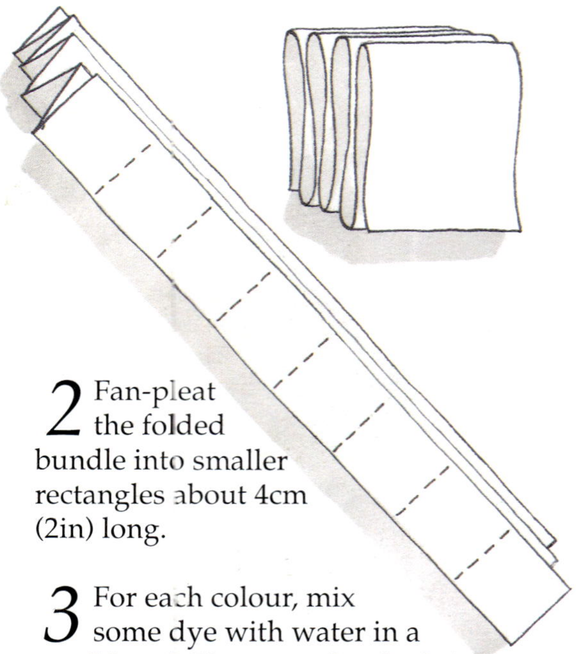

2 Fan-pleat the folded bundle into smaller rectangles about 4cm (2in) long.

3 For each colour, mix some dye with water in a small bowl. Use more dye for bright colours, less for pastels. Prepare more dye as you need it.

4 Dip a corner or edge of the rectangle quickly in one of the dyes to colour only a limited area.

5 After dipping, squeeze the extra dye back into the dye bath by pinching the paper between your thumb and forefinger (or with paper towels). Rinse your fingers in the bowl of clean water after each dipping. This prevents unwanted colour marks on the paper.

You will need:

White tissue paper (good quality)
Food colours (or fabric dyes)
Small bowls or plastic cups for the dyes
A bowl of clean water
Paper towels
Newspapers to protect the work surface and for drying dyed papers

Caution: All dyes must be handled with care. Food colours wash off and are the best to use when working with children. Before you begin, cover all surfaces and the floor with newspapers.

6 Dip the other corners or edges in the other colours.

7 Unfold the dyed paper into the long fan-pleated strip. Squeeze out some water by pressing it between layers of kitchen towels or newspaper. This helps you to unfold the paper completely. If it begins to tear, squeeze out more moisture.

8 If you like, you can smooth dyed papers by placing them between two sheets of newspaper and ironing them on a low setting.

Coloured Tissue Paper

You can vary the white backgrounds of dip-dyed papers by starting with pale-coloured tissue papers. For example, dipping a piece of pink paper into blue dye results in purple on a pink background.

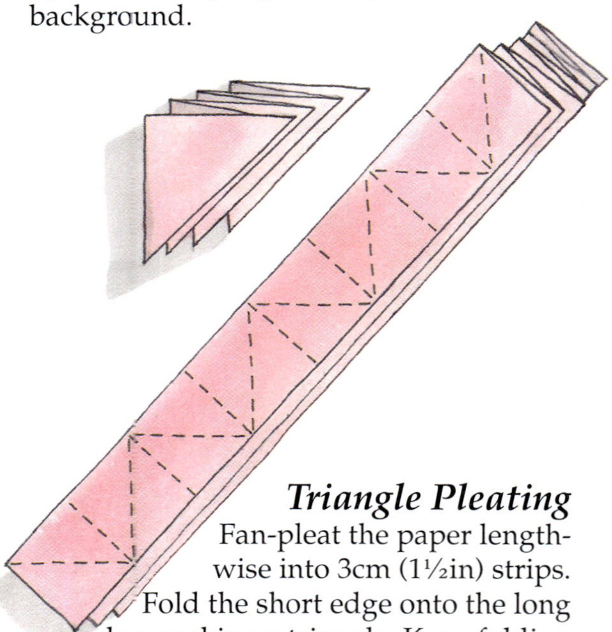

Triangle Pleating

Fan-pleat the paper lengthwise into 3cm (1½in) strips. Fold the short edge onto the long edge, making a triangle. Keep folding triangles for the whole length of the strip.

Other Effects

Experiment with folding the paper other ways. Try random folding or origami animals. Always dip the corners or edges. Fill in bare areas by dipping cotton swabs in the dye and painting on dots and stripes.

Cut paper into stars, circles and other shapes before folding and dipping. If the paper is dipped into water before dyeing, you will get softer outlines.

Greeting Cards and Gift Tags
Cut dyed paper into pieces and glue them onto blank cards or note cards.

Giftwrap
Wrap gifts with dyed paper, or wrap large packages with coloured tissue paper and paste a piece of dyed paper on top.

Other Papers
Experiment with other soft, absorbent papers. Papers with hard surfaces do not respond well. Try paper napkins and paper towels. Inexpensive Japanese 'rice' paper, which is sold in rolls at art supply stores, provides more elegant results.

Dyeing Circles

Bold circles and semi-circles can be dip-dyed by folding paper into rays. The two different results depend only on starting the creasing from two different corners. The dipping method is the same for both.

You will need:

Full size, half size or quarter size sheets of good quality white tissue paper
Dye baths of three or more different colours
Bowl of clean water, paper towels, newspapers to protect working surfaces

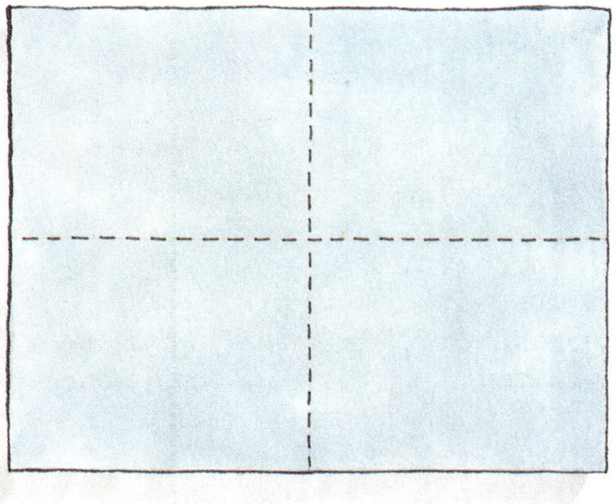

1 Fold a sheet of whatever size tissue paper you are using into quarters.

To Make Full Circles

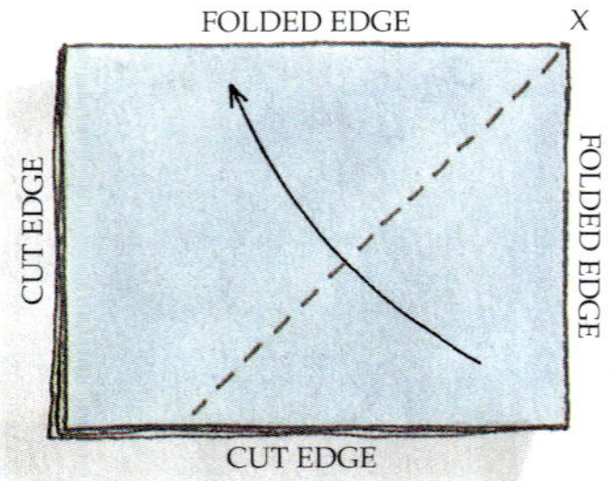

2 Note the position of the closed corner marked here with an X. Then bring the two folded edges together right through the middle of corner X. Crease.

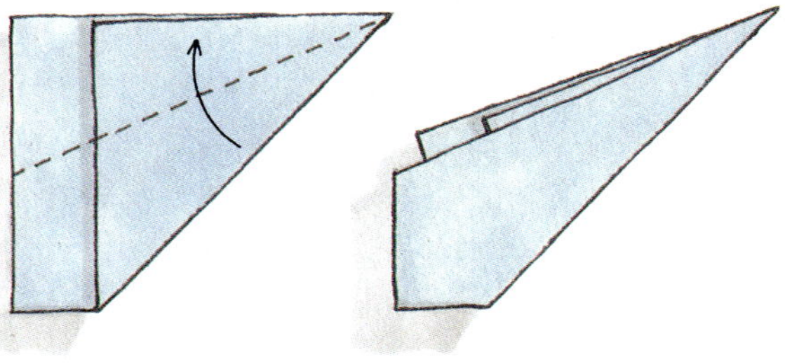

3 Bring the slanted edge to the long edge. Crease. Your folded ray is now ready for dipping (see step 6).

To Make Semi-Circles

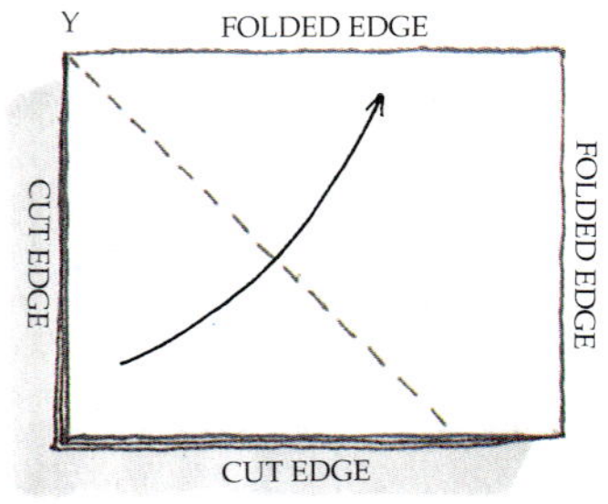

4 Note the position of the Y which falls between a folded edge and a cut edge. Bring two edges together right through the middle of corner Y. Crease.

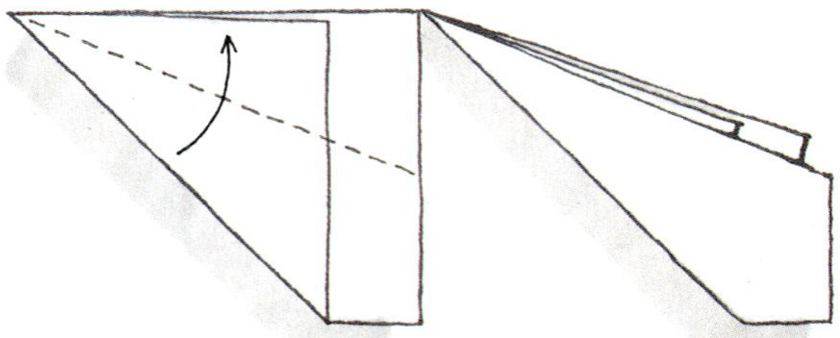

5 Bring the slanted edge to the long edge. Crease. Your folded ray is now ready for dipping.

Dipping

6 First dip a narrow corner. Then crease the paper 2cm (1in) away from the coloured part and dip the crease into another colour.

7 Unfold the crease and make another crease, again 2cm (1in) away from the coloured part and dip again. Experiment with more creases.

Paste Patterns

Decorating with paste is a method of colouring paper which is particularly suitable to do with children. Wallpaper paste is spread on the surface of the paper, then combed or pressed with small objects to produce delicate or bold designs.

1 Spread newspaper over your work surface. Mix the wallpaper paste, according to the directions on the package. It is better to make it a little thicker than too liquid. If the paste is lumpy, strain it through a sieve. Mix in the paint.

2 Brush the coloured paste over the paper.

3 Pattern the paste with the fork. If necessary you can correct the design by brushing over the paste and drawing a new pattern.

4 Dry the paper on newspaper.

Patterning Tools

Instead of a fork, scrape patterns with a stick, a teasing comb (with wide teeth) or make combs from cardboard. You can make your own comb by cutting a piece of cardboard about 5cm (2in) wide. Make angled cuts as shown. Experiment by cutting teeth wider apart, leaving narrow flat areas at the edge and varying the width of the teeth.

You can also pattern the paper with other hard objects such as bottle tops, corks and other things.

You will need:

Typing, computer and other kinds of paper
Wallpaper paste
Bowl for mixing paste
Small bowls or plastic cups when mixing more than one colour
Water soluble paints (tempera, watercolour or acrylic)
Brush or piece of sponge, 3cm (1in) or wider
Fork
Newspapers for covering work surface and on which to dry papers

Papers

As the original paper shows through your design, you can create interesting effects when you begin with coloured paper or foil giftwrap.

More Colours

Divide prepared wallpaper paste into small bowls or plastic cups, before colouring. Then add a different colour to each bowl. In this way you can make papers in various colours.

The technique of paste patterning was known as early as the 17th century, and became a popular home craft during Victorian times. It lost popularity during the latter half of the century, but is now enjoying a revival. Traditionally the patterned papers are seen in books as endpapers and for covering boxes, but they can also be used for notecards, giftwrap and in other ways.

Uses for Handmade Papers

Handmade papers lend themselves well to adding textured touches to writing papers, giftwrap and jewelry. The initial card, shown below, is an example of how you can cut papers, but try out some other forms as shown in the Mostly Cutting section. Folding involving perhaps one, two or three creases is also possible. Here are some specific ideas and they will probably suggest more possibilities to you.

Stationery, Thank-You Notes and Greetings Cards
Because of the nature of these handmade sheets, it is best to glue them on top of other papers, such as greetings cards. Paste on either a complete sheet or divide a sheet into several more or less equal-sized pieces and paste them on in a geometric pattern.

Initial Card
Cut out a letter of the alphabet from a sheet of handmade paper. Cut a piece of card wider and higher than the letter. Fold it in half. Glue the bottom of the letter to the front of the card. When the card stands up the top of the letter will be silhouetted.

Illustrated Cards
After you have prepared a greetings card as suggested, you can glue on an illustration. A photo or other illustration gains in importance when handled in this way, because the card acts like a frame. Consider a head shot, family group, holiday scene and other photos, a magazine illustration or cooking recipe which you would like to share with someone else.

Gift Tags
Make pieces of paper with a small mould, or cut larger sheets into smaller pieces.

Earrings
1 Place a pastry cutter of a star, heart or other shape on top of the screen in the mould.

2 Or cut a slice off a cardboard tube and use it like a pastry cutter.

3 Or use a tea strainer as the mould to form round paper.

4 Pour in the pulp. Couch and dry in the usual way. Cover the completed earrings with acrylic spray (see Protective Coatings, pages 12-13) and attach earring fittings.

Sachets
A perfumed sachet for keeping a lingerie drawer sweet-smelling can be prepared with a small piece of unsized handmade paper. Add a drop or two of perfume and you will have a small, but thoughtful, gift.

Books
Make several sheets of sized paper of the same size. Sew them together at the side.

Index